*Creating
a Professional
Learning Community
in Your School*

EDUCATORS AS
Learners

Edited by **Penelope J. Wald** and **Michael S. Castleberry**

ASCD

Association for Supervision and Curriculum Development
Alexandria, Virginia USA

Association for Supervision and Curriculum Development
1703 N. Beauregard St. • Alexandria, VA 22311-1714 USA
Telephone: 1-800-933-2723 or 703-578-9600 • Fax: 703-575-5400
Web site: http://www.ascd.org • E-mail: member@ascd.org

Gene R. Carter, *Executive Director*
Michelle Terry, *Associate Executive Director,*
   Program Development
Nancy Modrak, *Director, Publishing*
John O'Neil, *Director of Acquisitions*
Julie Houtz, *Managing Editor of Books*
Carolyn R. Pool, *Associate Editor*
Gary Bloom, *Director, Design and Production Services*

Karen Monaco, *Senior Designer*
Tracey A. Smith, *Production Manager*
Dina Murray, *Production Coordinator*
John Franklin, *Production Coordinator*
Valerie Sprague, *Desktop Publisher*
Tess Patrick, *Project Assistant*
Winfied Swanson, *Indexer*

This work was developed under Grant #HO2450038 from the Office of Special Education and Rehabilitation Services, U.S. Department of Education (OSERS/DOE), and sponsored by The George Washington University, Washington, D.C., in partnership with the Fairfax County Public Schools, Fairfax, Virginia. The content does not necessarily reflect the position or policy of OSERS/DOE, and no official endorsement of these materials should be inferred.

ASCD publications present a variety of viewpoints. The views expressed or implied in this book should not be interpreted as official positions of the Association.

Printed in the United States of America.

s02/2000

ASCD Stock No.: 100005
ASCD member price: $19.95   nonmember price: $23.95

Library of Congress Cataloging-in-Publication Data
Educators as learners : creating a professional learning community in
your school / edited by Penelope J. Wald and Michael S. Castleberry.
    p. cm.
Includes bibliographical references and index.
  ISBN 0-87120-366-9 (pbk.)
  1. Teachers—In-service training—United States—Case studies. I.
Wald, Penelope Jo. II. Castleberry, Michael S., 1945-
  LB1731 .E355 2000
  370'.71'5—dc21

                       99-050780

05 04   10 9 8 7 6 5 4 3 2

Creating a Professional Learning Community in Your School

EDUCATORS AS Learners

List of Figures · iv
Foreword *by Roland Barth* · v
Preface and Acknowledgments · · · · · · · · · · · · · · · · · · · vii

Part I. Cornerstones

1. Realigning for Change · 3
2. Learning Communities—An Ethos for Professional Change · · · · · · · · 7
3. Leading Professional Learning Communities · · · · · · · · · · · 18

Part II. Process

4. Identity of the Learning Community · · · · · · · · · · · · · · · 31
5. Learning as a Community · 43
6. Enhancing Capacity to Learn · · · · · · · · · · · · · · · · · · 59

Part III: Tools for Learning

Tool 1. Force Field Analysis · 79
Tool 2. Probable and Preferred Future · · · · · · · · · · · · · · · 82
Tool 3. Affinity · 85
Tool 4. Open Space · 87
Tool 5. Think, Pair, Share · 91
Tool 6. Communication Norms for Collaborative Groups · · · · · · · · 92
Tool 7. Left-Hand Column · 103
Tool 8. The Pyramid · 107
Tool 9. Ground Rules · 109
Tool 10. Communication Patterns · · · · · · · · · · · · · · · · · · 112

Epilogue · 116
Glossary · 119
References and Bibliography · 121
Index · 124
About the Editors and Contributors · · · · · · · · · · · · · · · · · 129

List of Figures

1.1. Building Professional Learning Communities · · · · · · · · · · · · · 5

2.1. Wheel of Learning · 11

4.1. Moments of Magic Chart · · · · · · · · · · · · · · · · · · 33

4.2. Histomap · 35

4.3. Context Mapping · 39

4.4. Current Snapshot · 41

4.5. Roller Coaster of Change · · · · · · · · · · · · · · · · · · 42

5.1. Collaborative Learning Process · · · · · · · · · · · · · · · 46

5.2. Time Line of the Collaborative Learning Process · · · · · · · · 47

5.3. Shared Meaning Chart · · · · · · · · · · · · · · · · · · · 49

5.4. Charter · 50

5.5. Game Plan · 51

5.6. Exploration Grid · 52

5.7. KWL Chart · 54

5.8. Action Plan Grid · 55

6.1. Sample Ground Rules for Meetings · · · · · · · · · · · · · 70

6.2. Sample Ground Rules for Brainstorming · · · · · · · · · · · 70

6.3. Task Roles That Support Group Functioning · · · · · · · · · 71

6.4. Trust Roles That Support Group Functioning · · · · · · · · · 72

6.5. Sample Meeting Agenda Notes · · · · · · · · · · · · · · · 73

6.6. Team Functioning Scale · · · · · · · · · · · · · · · · · · · 73

Tool 10. Diagram of Communication Patterns · · · · · · · · · · · 115

Foreword

By Roland Barth

"Our school is a community of learners!" How many times do we see and hear this assertion, now so common in public schools? This is an ambitious promissory note, indeed.

The promise, is, first, that the school is a "community," a place full of adults and youngsters who care about, look after, and root for one another and who work together for the good of the whole—in times of need as well as times of celebration. I find that precious few schools live up to this mantle of "community." Many more are simply organizations or institutions.

As if "community" were not enough to promise, a "community of learners" is much more. Such a school is a community whose defining, underlying culture is one of learning. A community of learners is a community whose most important condition for membership is that one be a learner—whether one is called a student, teacher, principal, parent, support staff, or certified staff. Everyone. A tall order to fill. And one to which all too few schools aspire, and even fewer attain.

The big message of this little volume lies in its title: *Educators as Learners: Creating a Professional Learning Community in Your School.*

For when the adults within the schoolhouse commit to the heady and hearty goal of promoting their own learning and that of their colleagues, several things follow: They leave the ranks of the senior, wise priesthood, the learned, and become first-class members of that community of learners. And when the adults come to take their own learning seriously, value and promote it, students take note. And when students see some of the most important role models in their lives learning, they too will learn, even *achieve*. Hence, adults' learning in our schools is a basic, not a frill.

Schools exist to promote the learning of all of their inhabitants. Indeed, the central purpose of a school is to invent and then to provide the conditions under which profound levels of human learning can flourish. That's why we have them. To paraphrase the legendary coach Vince Lombardi: "In schools, learning isn't the most important thing; it's the ONLY thing." So just how do you transform a

Roland S. Barth is the author of *The Principal Learner: A Work in Progress* (1997), *Improving Schools from Within* (1990), and *Run School Run* (1980). He is a former public school teacher and principal and member of the faculty at the Harvard Graduate School of Education. Barth was the founding director of the Harvard Principals' Center and of the International Network of Principals Centers.

school into a community of learners?

Educators as Learners offers nothing less than a "lesson plan" for members of a school or school system to transform their institution or organization into a learning community. By offering abundant, explicit, useful examples and case studies; rich activities; imaginative processes; and thoughtful commentary, this book provides a coherent roadmap that will go a long way in helping a school make good on the promise, "Our school is a community of learners."

Preface and Acknowledgments

Books don't just appear. Human desires and aspirations are forces that contribute to creating a book. This book resulted from several intersecting forces. First was the desire to bring into being a school-centered, future-focused change model for schools. In this change model, the protagonists are members of the school community—parents, teachers, specialists, children, and administrators. The direction of change is future oriented, with all members contributing to the explanation of who they are as a community, who they want to become, and how they can grow together.

A second force was the desire to reframe "learning" in our schools. Learning has long been the province of children in schools, yet we know that learning is as important to the life of a teacher as it is to the life of a student. If schools are to thrive in the 21st century, everyone in the schoolhouse must be a learner. Learning goes hand in hand with change, yet all too often schools are asked to change without giving staff the opportunity to learn.

The third desire was to offer a vehicle for educators to experience their passion for and love of teaching. Teaching is a profession of the heart. It arises from a deep calling to make a difference in the lives of children. But passions can subside and fires grow cold, especially in a climate where education has become the scapegoat for the ills of society. Michael Fullan, a well-known school reform activist, suggests that it is currently a bleak time in the field of education. He states, "Anyone who spends time in public schools can feel the growing, deepening malaise among educators, whether it stems from a sense on the part of teachers that the public and the government do not care about them or from an overwhelming sense of despair that the problems are insurmountable and worsening" (1997, p. 217). We need a process that renews and empowers teachers in their work.

Finally, we hope that the collaborative learning process will stimulate the ability of school communities to hear and act on the multiple perspectives of teachers, specialists, paraprofessionals, parents, and administrators. And out of this dialogue, new knowledge and practices will emerge that embrace the diversity of all the children attending our schools.

In this book, we describe an emergent model of professional development—a model where learning becomes a way of life for educators as well as children; where collaboration among teachers, parents, and administrators is key to creating positive results for all children; and where leadership relies on vision, values, and relationships. Professional development literature reports the positive effect of professional learning communities on teacher resiliency and student learning. Yet knowledge about how to support the emergence of professional learning communities is rudimentary. This book offers a beginning theoretical framework and practical guidance for thinking about why and how to build professional learning communities in schools.

☛   ☛   ☛

Educators as Learners: Creating a Professional Learning Community in Your School emerged from the work of Project REALIGN, a national model inservice training project. Funded by the U.S. Department of Education from 1995 to 1998, Project REALIGN was sponsored by The George Washington University Department of Teacher Preparation and Special Education in partnership with Fairfax County (Virginia) Public Schools. The intent of this professional development model was to deepen the capacity of adults in schools—that is, teachers, specialists, paraprofessionals, administrators, and parents—to function as powerful professional learning communities committed to creating new strategies for meeting the diverse needs of all students in their schools. Project REALIGN staff worked with approximately 150 parents, administrators, and teaching staff representing multiple roles, disciplines, and grade levels at five public elementary schools in Fairfax County, Virginia.

Over the three years of Project REALIGN, a multitude of outstanding educators contributed their time, intellect, and hearts to giving birth to this professional development model. First, the Project REALIGN staff, a group of hard-working risk takers, weathered many a storm as we worked together to develop our ideas. Many thanks go to Andrea Sobel, Holly Blum, Elaine Barker, and Maret Wahab.

The actual writing of this book was accomplished by a wondrous team of educators. Some team members were involved in the initial conceptualization of the book, and some participated in the rewriting process. All played an important part in articulating the ideas found in this book. The contributing authors are Laura Bell, Holly Blum, Amy King, Andrea Sobel, Maret Wahab, Karren Wood, and Ramona Wright. Others, such as Muriel Farley, Marianne Latall, Marie Celeste, Esther Merves, Sheryl Fahey, and Renna Jordan, helped shape and refine our ideas.

Many educators in the Fairfax County Public Schools, who worked as facilitators in Project REALIGN, helped "tease out" the important elements of this model. Thank you to Wendy Boehm, Marty Brosky, Maura Burke, Karen Bump, Liz Bush, Thea Cox, Carol Flicker, Laura Freeman, Pam Pavuk, Jennifer Rose, Donna Schatz, and Jean Waylonis for their insightful questions, comments, and contributions to REALIGN.

Other communities instrumental in the development of this model were the parents, teaching staffs, and administrators at elementary schools where we piloted this professional development model—Stratford Landing, Clearview, Keene Mill, Fairfax Villa, and Hayfield. We are grateful for their dedication to quality practices, their patience, and their feedback.

Finally, we are forever indebted to our editor Ellie Abrams and her wonderful staff for their endless hours of poring over the manuscript and crafting it into a final product. We also would like to thank our colleagues at The

George Washington University Department of Teacher Preparation and Special Education Infant and Early Childhood Programs who provided a support system and cheering section for the work of REALIGN.

Out of this large, committed community, a budding model for professional development has emerged. We hope this book will challenge your thinking as much as it did ours.

Penelope J. Wald
Project REALIGN, Project Director

Michael S. Castleberry
Project REALIGN, Principal Investigator

Washington, D.C.
February 2000

Cornerstones

Part I introduces concepts and assumptions that are instrumental to building school-based professional learning communities. Chapter 1, "Realigning for Change," presents a theoretical model for change in education, based on schools as collaborative communities.

Chapter 2, "Learning Communities: An Ethos for Professional Change," discusses the role of collegial learning as a renewing force in schools during times of change. Here, we compare the active-interactive, learning-community approach to professional development with the more traditional "expert" training approach. In this chapter, we present emerging assumptions and a conceptual frame for professional learning communities.

Chapter 3, "Leading Professional Learning Communities," focuses on leadership qualities that support the building of professional learning communities in our schools. In this chapter, we explore the leadership qualities of vision, values, service, capacity building, and relationship building, along with snapshots of school leaders in action.

1

Realigning for Change

A teacher can never truly teach unless she is learning herself.
A lamp can never light another flame unless it continues to burn its own flame.

—RABINDRANATH TRAGORE (1861–1941), NOBEL PRIZE LAUREATE FOR LITERATURE

The Need for Change

In the quest for school improvement, change initiatives have overwhelmed the system. Several decades ago, schools might have had one initiative every year or two—mostly in the form of textbook adoptions. Now schools are struggling to coordinate multiple initiatives that are simultaneously stacked one on top of another. Each brings an answer to a problem—the technology initiative, the literacy initiative, the safe schools initiative—but together they create overwhelmed and overworked staff and a potentially fragmented education for students.

How did education decide on this additive, piecemeal approach to school improvement? This predisposition to improve things by reorganizing the pieces, adding new pieces, and taking out ineffective pieces dates back to the Newtonian mechanistic worldview of the 17th century. The Newtonian model was built on the idea that the world could be controlled like a big machine (Caine & Caine, 1997). By the 1800s, this mechanistic imagery had influenced not only our thinking in the sciences but also our thinking about organizations. Youngblood (1997), in *Life at the Edge of Chaos,* comments on this mechanistic perception of organizations:

> Normally we view organizations as machines with parts that we can disassemble and reconstruct in any fashion we wish. Organizational change is frequently an exercise in moving parts around until we achieve the magic formula that produces the performance results we desire. We expect to be able to predict the outcomes of these changes and to control them completely (p. 76).

It is no surprise that education adopted this predictable, orderly, bureaucratic model of functioning. After all, the charge of the public education system was to provide education to

3

the masses—a task that resembled the mass production that was going on in our factories. So our schools were divided into grade levels, with each grade assigned specific pieces of the curriculum and a teacher to teach it. When pieces of the system failed, the leaders isolated the problem and replaced the broken piece or added another piece to make the system more effective. In this way we got more curriculum, more specialists, and more supervisors.

Dramatic social, economic, and political changes have occurred since this system of education was originally conceived. Diversity, mobility, and technology have emerged as prime forces shaping our daily lives—forces that were minimal to nonexistent 50 years ago. Yet our schools are still laboring under the same bureaucratic mode of organization. What we have is an educational dinosaur, slow to move and unable to adapt, living in a world of rapid-fire change.

It is time for our system of education to change. We no longer need schools designed to educate children "en masse." We need schools that prepare our learners to lead productive lives in this complex, high-tech, and fast-changing world—schools that are responsive, fluid, and adaptive to emerging needs and opportunities. The next generation of schools must have the capacity for continuous renewal. We must have an ethos that values lifelong learning for staff and families, as well as students.

A New Model for Professional Development in Schools

This book presents ways to create dynamic learning communities for the adults in our schools—communities where individual and organizational growth occurs simultaneously. Two cornerstones of this professional development model are (1) schools as communities and (2) collaborative learning.

The concept of *schools as communities* provides the context for growth and change—the fertile ground for growth to occur. A school community is a composite of people representing many ages, roles, backgrounds, and dreams. Members of the community are aligned around common goals, shared values, and an agreed-on way of being and doing. This alignment of ideology forms the unique identity of community. It is from this ideological base that communities take action. It is through this community of mind that synergy arises.

Collaborative learning, the second cornerstone of this model, offers a process for simultaneously promoting individual and organizational capacity building. Collaborative learning assumes a shared focus, a shared responsibility to learn, and a disciplined approach to acquiring the desired goal. It demands that individuals shed the expert role and adopt a collaborative approach that recognizes the values, knowledge, and expertise of all community members. The collaborative learning process engages members of the community in a cycle of exploring, experimenting, and reflecting relative to a specific outcome. The knowledge and skills that are generated through collaborative inquiry enriches the knowledge base of the school. From this bank of knowledge and expertise, improved programs and services are born.

The concepts of "schools as communities" and "collaborative learning" interact like an ever-expanding web (see Figure 1.1). The core of the web contains the school community's values, visions, and ways of relating. Collaborative learning represents the potential for growth and capacity building. Multiple opportunities for collaborative learning exist within a community. Community members are free to self-organize around topics of interest to them, yet they are guided by their community's core ideology. The result is a professional learning community connected by shared values and visions while nourished by high levels of energy and forward movement emanating from the work of multiple, self-organized, collaborative learning groups.

This book does not dwell on fixing current problems in our schools, but rather on creating a new future for school communities. John Gardner (1964) in *Self-Renewal* underscores the need for this future-focused approach to organizational renewal:

> No society is likely to renew itself unless its dominant orientation is to the future. There is a readily discernible difference between the society that is oriented to the future and the one

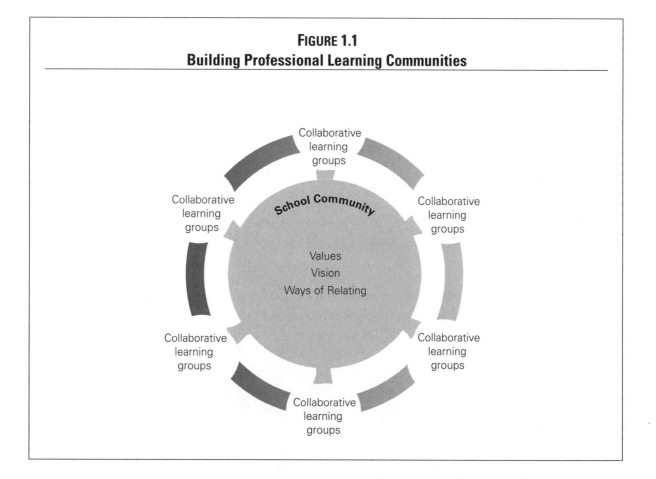

FIGURE 1.1
Building Professional Learning Communities

that is oriented to the past. Some individuals and societies look forward and have the future ever in mind, others are preoccupied with the past and are antiquarian in their interests. The former have a vivid sense of what they are becoming, the latter a vivid sense of what they have been. The former are fascinated by the novelty of each day's experience, the latter have a sense of having seen everything (p. 105).

With this work, we are forging into the future; and we invite you to join us in this collaborative learning adventure.

Learning Communities—An Ethos for Professional Change

During my 25 years as an educator, I have focused on one thing—the mastery of the content I need to teach. I am certain that if I know the content well enough, then I can deliver it in a way that anyone and everyone can learn the information. I work very hard to master the content in all my subject areas. To learn new content, I leave my school (after a full day of work or after writing a full day of lesson plans) to attend a training workshop, a conference, or a course. Most often I attend training sessions where experts in the subject area have a limited amount of time to transfer all their knowledge about the subject to me and 100 other teachers. They may use a lecture approach combined with demonstrations and guided practice during the training session.

After attending the event, I return to my classroom, shut my door, try the new stuff with my kids, and, if I am diligent, make adjustments based on feedback to myself. Seldom do I receive a follow-up call from the district staff development office, on-site coaching from the trainer, or even a "how's it going" from the building administrator. Sometimes I just give up if the new approach doesn't seem to be working. Most often, I am off to another workshop to hear about something else new before I have a chance to really think through and use what I last "learned."

This scenario is fictitious, but it reflects the reality of the traditional training approach to professional development. Harrison (1995) describes training as the process for transferring to the employee the knowledge and skills that the organization has decided the employee needs to know. That description is fairly consistent with what happens in education. The state, the district, or the school administrator determines the knowledge and skills a teacher needs to know and provides training to impart that knowledge to the teacher. The teacher then is responsible for delivering the information to the students. And, finally, the students are graded on how much they absorb. That's the *training food chain*.

We see this inservice approach in many school districts across the United States. It assumes that professional development is effective and efficient when it is

• planned and delivered by the school district;

• conducted in large groups at off-site training events; and

• led by experts who transmit knowledge, skills, and strategies to selected staff.

Yet its ability to prepare staff to meet the increasing demands in education is becoming more and more questionable. The 1996 National Foundation for Improvement in Education (NFIE) publication, *Teachers Take Charge of Their Learning*, enumerates the long list of demands on educators.

> Today's teachers must be sensitive to varying social demands and expectations; must be able to diagnose and address the individual learning and development needs of students, including special emotional, physical, social and cognitive needs; must be able to use information technologies in all aspects of their work; must make important decisions about what and how much to teach of the overwhelming amount of new knowledge being created in every field; and must reach out more effectively to parents and the community than ever before (p. xiv).

During the past decade, education literature has promoted a new set of staff development practices, such as teacher inquiry, action research, professional collaboration, and learning communities to help educators meet these rising expectations. Much of the writing contains sharp contrasts between the traditional training approach and the "next generation" of practices. For example, in *Leadership for the Schoolhouse* (1996), Thomas Sergiovanni addresses the need for teacher inquiry and discourse:

> Few axioms are more fundamental than the one that acknowledges the link between what happens to teachers and what happens to students.

Inquiring classrooms, for example, are not likely to flourish in schools where inquiry among teachers is discouraged. A commitment to problem solving is difficult to instill in students who are taught by teachers for whom problem solving is not allowed. Where there is little discourse among teachers, discourse among students will be harder to promote and maintain. The idea of making classrooms into learning communities for students will remain more rhetoric than real unless schools become learning communities for teachers too (p. 139).

The question then becomes, How are we going to get from the traditional training approach to one that embraces schools as learning communities for educators? To understand the path to this new paradigm, we first need to become familiar with the key assumptions that underlie the concepts of "learning" and "community."

Looking at Adult Learning

Creating a professional development system that supports school improvement and professional renewal must be grounded in sound assumptions of adult learning (Loucks-Horsley, 1995). Many times we act as if learning happens as a direct result of exposure to new information; as if at the moment of hearing new information, we "learn" it. Learning is much more complex than that, especially when the goal of learning is to build the capacity of the individual or the system. Five assumptions about adult learning are central to building professional learning communities.

Assumptions About Adult Learning

- Inquiry into underlying assumptions deepens the learning process.
- Learning is an active process that occurs over time.
- Learning is driven by the learner around meaningful issues.
- Learning is experimental by nature.
- Learning is fueled by rich, diverse, accessible sources of information.

Assumption 1. Inquiry into underlying assumptions deepens the learning process.

Since John Dewey first distinguished between thinking and rote learning, learning theorists have elaborated on the claim that there are different kinds of learning. Senge (1990) describes two types of learning: adaptive and generative learning.

- *Adaptive learning* has three main steps: (1) A problem is encountered, (2) solutions are identified, and (3) solutions are applied. The adaptive model operates from a set of assumptions, beliefs, and interpretations. These assumptions form a box or framework for viewing the problem. Within this framework, a discrete number of solutions are possible. The inquiry centers around the question "What should we do?" The solution relies on our ability to recall past solutions and apply them to the present situation. It is a process of "recollecting" and "reapplying" information.
- *Generative learning* emphasizes a creative, "out-of-the-box" approach to thinking and learning. It begins the same way as adaptive learning—a problem is encountered. But rather than jumping into action with the question "What should we do?" we slow down and ask, "Why is this a problem?" or "What do we believe or assume that makes this a problem?" This new question leads us to look at the assumptions or way of thinking that created the problem, and challenges us to reconsider the validity of those assumptions.

Inquiry into the assumptions and beliefs that create the problem is an essential element of generative learning. Daniel Kim (1994) maintains that we don't realize that our problems occur in the context of our assumptions. For example, being unmarried is a problem when the predominate assumption is that people who are not married must be uninteresting and unattractive. It is not a problem when the predominate assumption is that the best and brightest people tend to be unmarried. In schools, having 30 children in a class is a problem when the predominant assumption is that one teacher has the sole responsibility for the education of all 30 children. This may not be a problem if the predominate assumption is that a class of 30 students has two teachers and a double-sized classroom. Once we realize that people view information differently because they operate from different beliefs and assumptions (what is a problem to one person may be a blessing to another), we can work at seeing the situation from different perspectives. In this way, we open up new ways of thinking and acting.

In education, the capacity for generative learning greatly enhances professional development. The inquiry approach, with its emphasis on examining the relationship between theory

A Situation from Two Perspectives

Johnny is doodling while his teacher, Ms. Adaptive, is introducing a new science concept. Doodling during a lecture is a problem for her. She decides to discuss it with Ms. Generative. "I'm having a problem with Johnny doodling during my science lectures; I think I should take his pencil away." This is an example of a problem-solution or adaptive-learning approach. Doodling is the problem and removing the stimulus, the pencil, is the solution.

Ms. Generative suggests, "Let's not jump to a solution. Let's think about why we consider Johnny's doodling a problem."

"Because doodling distracts children from learning," replies Ms. Adaptive. That's the assumption that created the problem. Now the assumption is out in the open, and the teachers are able to discuss it.

"Is it true that doodling interferes with learning?" asks Ms. Generative. She continues, "Maybe, maybe not. It may help Johnny to focus. Rather than ignore what might be his learning style, we could help him learn to doodle more purposefully, using graphic webbing to represent what is being said. What other ideas could we come up with if we operated from the assumption that doodling is *not* a problem?" This is an example of generative thinking—an examination of the problem at the assumption level, not the action or solution level.

and practice, supports the generative learning process. Darling-Hammond (1997) argues that quality professional development is "centered around the critical activities of teaching and learning; grows from investigations of practice; and is built upon substantial professional discourse" (p. 323). It is becoming more and more obvious that the professional development models in the 21st century will draw on the skills of inquiry and generative thinking (Sagor, 1995; Sparks & Hirsh, 1997).

Assumption 2. Learning is an active process that occurs over time.

Learning involves a constant movement back and forth between thinking and action (O'Neil, 1995). The learner not only hears and processes the information but also experiments with it and then documents and reflects on the results. Handy (1995) describes the learning process as a *cyclical* process of questioning, developing ideas, testing, and reflecting—forming a "wheel of learning" (see Figure 2.1).* The learner moves sequentially through the four quadrants of the wheel of learning:

• A problem that needs a solution triggers the learner to ask questions.
• The learner gathers ideas that answer the question and selects the most feasible idea.
• The learner tries out the idea and tests it.
• The learner reflects on the results to decide if the idea is a satisfactory solution to the problem.

---

*From *Learning Organizations*, edited by Sarita Chawla and John Renesch. Copyright (c) 1995 by Productivity, Inc., P.O. Box 13390, Portland, OR 97213-0390; phone: 1-800-394-6868. Reprinted by permission.

FIGURE 2.1
Wheel of Learning

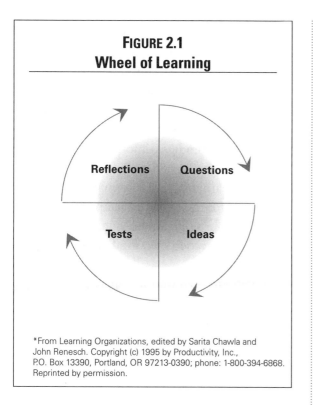

Reflections Questions

Tests Ideas

*From Learning Organizations, edited by Sarita Chawla and John Renesch. Copyright (c) 1995 by Productivity, Inc., P.O. Box 13390, Portland, OR 97213-0390; phone: 1-800-394-6868. Reprinted by permission.

The wheel of learning substantiates the importance of job-embedded learning. Learning occurs when people actually try new ideas. The place for that to happen is on the job. *Teachers Take Charge* emphasizes the need for ongoing on-the-job learning opportunities:

> The learning that teachers need from each other is learning that continues throughout the day, the school year, and the career. It is the constant improvement of practice based on observation, feedback, reflection, evaluation, and concerted effort to try again with something new (NFIE, 1996, pp. 34–35).

Assumption 3. Learning is driven by the learner around meaningful issues.

The motivation to learn begins inside oneself with a need or a question. Learning emerges from an intrinsic desire to know. When learning starts from within the learner, it becomes a generative process in which the learner seeks to create something new—to bring an idea or a strategy into being.

Sergiovanni's (1996) renewal approach to professional development capitalizes on the teacher's personal need to know and commitment to excellence, rather than on external goals. In this approach, professional development is driven by intrinsic forces rather than by external ones. When considering this staff-centered approach to teacher development, Bolin (1987) asks:

> What would happen if we set aside the question of how to improve the teacher and looked instead at what we can do to encourage the teacher? Asking how to encourage the teacher places the work of improvement in the hands of the teacher. It presupposes that the teacher desires to grow, to be self-defining, and to engage in teaching as a vital part of life (p. 11).

We need systems that empower staff to define their professional path and grow in ways that are meaningful in their work with students.

Assumption 4. Learning is experimental by nature.

Learning requires a degree of initiative and risk taking in the face of uncertainty. It is experimental by nature. The learner must be patient and forgiving because learning is a trial-and-error process, and mistakes are inevitable.

Obstacles to learning abound, especially for adult learners. One is the fear of being viewed as incompetent by one's peers. Continuing to flounder is often less threatening than turning to colleagues for help. Embarrassment is often associated with learning as an adult. When we lack knowledge, we are often left feeling stupid and vulnerable. Or there may be the fear of reprisal from people in "higher" positions of authority if they identify our incompetencies or if we make mistakes. Ironically, we learned many of these risk-avoidance behaviors from our experiences in schools. We *must* create environments where our fears won't be reproduced in our students.

In teaching, we often find a bias for *action*. Once a problem is identified, we immediately seek a solution. Time for exploring and reflecting is lost in the push to act. It takes courage and willpower for us—as individuals or groups—to slow down and look more completely at the problem, at the assumptions behind the problem, and at the desired results.

Assumption 5. Learning is fueled by rich, diverse, and accessible sources of information.

> For a system to remain alive . . . information must be continually generated. The fuel of life is new information. . . . If there is nothing new or if the information that exists merely confirms what is, the result will be death (Wheatley, 1992, pp. 104–105).

A vital learning environment offers rich resources. The resources come in many forms and can be accessed in multiple ways. Colleagues, experts, literature, and technology present different options that appeal to different learning styles. In this new professional development paradigm, information flows in many directions. In addition to the traditional expert-to-learner flow of information, opportunities exist for the expert to learn from the learner and for the learners to learn from each other and from their own fund of knowledge and experience.

The traditional training approach described in the beginning of this chapter is one method for providing staff with useful, relevant information about current education issues. As a method of disseminating information, it has a permanent place in the staff development protocol.

Yet other rich and diverse sources of information can be found inside and outside the school walls. Inside the school walls, a strong predisposition must exist for sharing know-how and ideas among staff, for discussing success and failures, and for supporting each other in experimenting and reflecting. Going outside the school affords staff the opportunities to visit exemplary programs; network with other teachers; access consultants and university faculty; and tap into multiple forms of technology, such as video, computer, and telecommunications. This inside-outside approach to gathering information provides a balance between germinating the seeds within the school and cross-pollinating among schools and programs to stay connected and avoid the rigidity of thinking that often occurs when schools become too insular in their approach.

Contemplating Community

> We apply [the term *community*] to almost any collection of individuals—regardless of how poorly those individuals communicate with each other. It is a false use of the word. If we are going to use the word meaningfully, we must restrict it to a group of individuals who have learned how to communicate honestly with each other, whose relationships go deeper into their masks of composure, and who have developed some significant commitment to rejoice together, mourn together, delight in each other, and make others' conditions our own (Peck, 1987, p. 59).

Communities are "collections of individuals who are bounded together by natural will and who are together bound to a set of shared ideas and ideals. This bounding and binding is tight enough to transform them from a collection of 'I's' to a collective 'we'" (Sergiovanni, 1996, p. 48). When we apply the concept of community to schools, the focus shifts from school structure to school culture, from ways of organizing to ways of being, from brick and mortar to ideals and relationships.

Fullan (1998) argues that school reform has failed because of the focus on restructuring schools, that is, changing the ways schools are organized to improve teaching and learning. Hoping to find the right answer, schools have continuously adopted the latest curriculum and instructional delivery formulations, leaving staff exhausted by change and often still facing the original problems. Fullan advises us to look instead to the reculturing process—changing the norms, values, and relationships in our schools—as a more expedient way to improve

teaching and learning. He believes that fostering a more collaborative, collegial workplace among teachers will positively affect student outcomes. Rather than having new structures drive the change process, a change in culture toward a more collaborative, community-minded way of being together will dictate the necessary organizational changes in schools.

Examining assumptions underlying the concept of a community illuminates how a professional development approach focused on school culture rather than school structure could impact our schools. This section explores three assumptions about community.

Assumptions About Community:

- A shared philosophy bonds a community.
- A community is a web of diverse relationships.
- A community provides the context for the emergence of unpredictable potential.

Assumption 1. A shared philosophy bonds a community.

One of the most important actions for a school community is to develop a shared philosophy—an agreed-upon statement about child development, learning, and important outcomes for children. This shared philosophy (1) serves as a concrete document that guides the actions of all members of the school community—teachers, administrators, parents, and students—and (2) offers the school community a collective strength of mind and spirit. According to Saphier and D'Auria (1993), "The collective power of a school faculty united behind a few important commonly prized outcomes for students is virtually unlimited" (p. 3). A shared philosophy gives a school community a strong sense of identity and continuity in times of change. This philosophy is the compass for the school.

Shared purpose and values do not emerge out of a vision-building exercise or even a two-day faculty retreat. A school works at articulating and actualizing its most deeply felt beliefs over time. This process requires continual vigilance. Vigilance is present when purpose and values guide the ongoing conversations in the schoolhouse—when alignment exists between the day-to-day decisions and a community's expressed beliefs. Shared purpose and values serve to enhance the cohesiveness among staff, connect the school community to its higher purpose, and reenergize staff when the going gets rough.

Revisiting the school's philosophy is essential as staff members grow together and probe deeper into the beliefs that guide their actions. As Wheatley and Kellner-Rogers (1996) state:

> As we act together . . . our identity grows and evolves. It helps periodically to question what we have become. . . . Do we each organize our work from the same shared sense of what is significant? Such an inquiry helps return us to the energy and passion of that space of early vision. We return to the place where our community took form (p. 62).

Purpose and values are matters of the heart. As we come to discover more of who we are, our purpose and values become more visible in our words and actions. They become the organizer of our community. Our structure evolves from our purpose and values.

Assumption 2. A community is a web of diverse relationships.

> When we reach into the most fundamental basis of our being, we find a pregnant void, a web of relationships. When somebody asks us to talk about ourselves, we talk about family, work, academic background, sports affiliations, etc. In all this talk, where is our "self"? The answer is nowhere because the self is not a thing, but . . . a narrative striving to connect with other narratives and become richer (Kofman & Senge, 1993, p. 14).

Margaret Wheatley (1992), in *Leadership and the New Sciences*, suggests that we exist only in relationship to another person or idea. The constitution of the self happens in relationship, and relationship is at the heart of a community. Communities support certain ways of being and discourage others. As we work to build vital communities in our schools, the way we regard one another matters. Do we see each other as human beings brimming with possibility and potential or as part of an assembly line? The work of a community is to affirm who we are as individuals and who we can become together. We are gifts to one another. Our diversity adds richness to what we can offer each other. In schools, the work of the community begins when staff are able to meet face to face and identify the unique gifts and talents that each person brings to the situation. When staff from different classrooms, grade levels, and specialties come together, misunderstandings can be addressed; a commonality of vision, goals, and practices emerges; and dynamic synergy of thought and action is ignited.

To thrive on the diversity, community members must be able to effectively probe into each other's thinking. A community rich with diversity must be skilled at transforming controversy into a deeper understanding of the problem or issue at hand. Stephanie Ryan (1995) eloquently expresses the potential of diversity within a community. "The sense of community—where an appreciation of interrelatedness, our wholeness, allows for differences to be expressed and transcended graciously—offers fertile ground for learning and collaboration" (p. 289). Communities are webs of diverse relationship. The health of the community is reflected in how it welcomes and nurtures the expression of its diversity.

Assumption 3. A community provides the context for the emergence of unpredictable potential.

> Emergence is the surprising capacity we discover only when we join together. . . . We witness emergence any time we are surprised by a group's accomplishments or by our own achievements within a group (Wheatley & Kellner-Rogers, 1996, p. 67).

Community as a context for the *emergence of unpredictable potential* demands that each member be committed to high personal standards, lifelong learning, and the work of the community. All members are accountable for their contribution to the whole and have a sense of the relationship between themselves and the whole. Like a musician in an orchestra, members of the community are expected to be masterful in their own right while at the same time mindful of their role and the role of the others in creating the dynamic potential of the whole.

People form powerful communities when individuals realize they need one another to accomplish their work. They cannot accomplish the work alone. Members of these communities are "critically dependent on each other . . . where collaborative learning is not just nice but necessary to survival. This interdependence promises an atmosphere of joint responsibility, mutual respect, and a sense of personal and group identity" (Brown, 1994, p. 19).

This sense of interdependency feeds the potency of the collective. A community that sets extraordinary challenges for itself—challenges that no one person can handle alone and that require the discipline and commitment of each member—begins to radiate a new sense of energy and power.

Learning communities in schools harness the collective energy of staff for growth and change. The accomplishments of teachers working as individuals, good as they may be, pale in comparison to the accomplishments of a united faculty. It is like the difference between a bunch of good basketball players and an outstanding basketball team. The *synergy* that emerges from groups of teachers learning together and helping one another holds great potential for both improving student outcomes and creating a caring, nurturing environment among the staff (Joyce & Calhoun, 1995). The following statements, extracted directly from school reform literature, express the power of professional collaboration available to our schools.

Collaborating staff . . . relish opportunities to share ideas about teaching. They learn to appreciate the collegial interdependencies in ways that reach deep into the heart of their schools and classrooms and perceive individual and group risk-taking as learning opportunities (Uhl, 1995, p. 258).

Teachers' participation in a professional community of like-minded colleagues had a powerful effect on their ability to know better what to do in the classroom and to adapt their teaching strategies to more effectively meet student needs. Where such collegiality is high, teachers have more positive views of teaching and teach more successfully (Sergiovanni, 1996, p. 141).

The concept of community speaks of shared philosophy, networks of relationships, and synergy. It is a living, breathing context for organizing—a context where people, not tasks, occupy center stage. The concept of community offers a new place to start when creating a culture that supports the growth of educators.

☙ ☙ ☙

Literature offers definitions of learning communities that call forth our lofty and poetic side. For example, Kofman and Senge (1993) picture learning communities as

> spaces for generative conversations and concerted action [where] people can talk from their hearts and connect with one another in the spirit of dialogue. Their dialogue weaves a common ongoing fabric and connects them at the deep level of being. When people talk and listen to each other this way, they create a field of alignment that

produces tremendous power to invent new realities in conversation and bring about these new realities in action (p. 16).

To some, this description may be inspirational. To others, it may be too idealistic. Regardless of what we think about the concept of the learning community, we know the professional development compass is pointing in the direction of increased collegiality, collaboration, and ongoing inquiry. Michael Fullan, a leader in school reform, heralds in this new era with these words:

> The future of the world is a learning future . . . . It is a world where we will need generative concepts and capacities. What will be needed is the individual as inquirer and learner, mastery and know-how as prime strategies . . . teamwork and shared purpose which accepts both individualism and collectivism as essential to organizational learning (1993a, pp. vii–viii).

The traditional training approach is no longer the answer. Consensus is building around the notion that effective teaching in the 21st century will require "teachers, school administrators, and communities to join together to make all schools learning organizations and all teachers learners" (NFIE, 1996, p. xii). Professional learning communities have the potential to be a major catalyst in transforming the teaching-learning process because teachers, as members of a learning community, can experience learning in the same ways that their children should experience learning.

The concepts and assumptions associated with learning and community discussed in this chapter are equally applicable for teachers as they are for children. In this new paradigm, as we reflect on ourselves as learners in a larger community, we will better understand how our children feel as learners in similar situations. We will have new insights about cooperative learning in heterogeneous groups, learner-centered teaching, and the inquiry-based approach to learning because we will have had the experience firsthand as part of a learning community. We will be active participants in a world that is a learning world for everyone. And we will be all the wiser for it.

Leading Professional Learning Communities

A weaver is intrigued by an opportunity to create a tapestry that represents the varied qualities of leadership. To begin the intricate tapestry, the weaver carefully selects thread colors: bright orange for commitment, deep green for relationships, mustard yellow for trust, and ripe red for collaboration. With nimble fingers, the weaver adds a sea blue thread for values and a steel gray thread for service. Carefully woven into the pattern, each thread contributes beautifully to the increasing complexity of the tapestry. The combination of all the colors is inspiring to all who behold it. Last, a thread of black is woven around the perimeter of the tapestry. This sum of all colors represents the vision that frames and links each of the colors.

The tapestry is a holistic image of quality leadership. The weaver neither followed nor suggested a formula or exact proportions of colors. Each tapestry of leadership created by the weaver represents a leader's unique blend and arrangement of qualities. Although researchers have documented many characteristics of inspiring and effective leaders, we focus here on the five qualities of leadership that we found critical to building and sustaining professional learning communities in schools: vision, values, service, capacity building, and relationship building. The chapter includes five case studies—one for each quality. The case studies represent fictitious schools, yet they are based on the experiences of the authors as they worked with various elementary schools.

Past, Present, and Future

> Time present and time past
> Are both present in time future
> And time future contained in time present.
> —T. S. ELIOT (1888–1965),
> "BURNT NORTON" FROM *FOUR QUARTETS*

Over the years many schools have functioned under a hierarchical, command-and-control model of leadership that evolved during the industrial revolution. This era valued efficiency, predictability, control, and uniform mass production of goods, all of which became the earmarks of a successful organization and its leadership. The roles and actions of school leaders were, for the most part, congruent with the purpose of these 20th century industrial age schools: to systematically, uniformly, and efficiently provide students with the knowledge and skills necessary to function effectively in an industrial, democratic society.

As we enter the 21st century, our schools must continue to prepare our children to become productive citizens in a democratic society; and at the same time we must remember that we no longer live in the industrial age. We now live in a technologically sophisticated information age in which knowledge, not goods, is the prize product; fast-paced change, not stability, is the status quo; and futures are created, not predicted. For example, as recently as 1968, change was perceived as a predictable event; and now, just 30 years later, this view of change is significantly altered. Experience has taught us that change is a continuous journey.

In *What Matters Most: Teaching for America's Future*, the National Commission of Teaching and America's Future (1996) gives us this warning:

> There has been no previous time in history when the success, indeed the survival of nations and people, has been so tied to their ability to learn. Today's society has little room for those who cannot read, write, and compute proficiently; find and use resources; frame and solve problems; and continually learn new technologies, skills, and occupations. Every school must be organized to support powerful teaching and learning (p. 3).

To approach this challenge, we need leaders of school communities who are committed to continuous schoolwide learning and growing. We need leaders who can challenge both students and professionals and can transform our schools into powerful learning communities.

Building vital professional learning communities in schools asks the leader to perform a multitude of complex roles; these roles attend as much to realizing potential and creating relationships at both the individual and organizational level as they do to producing results. In much the same way as a painter carefully combines the colors of the palate to create a background from which the painting emerges, the leader creates a culture that serves as the setting for the emergence of a vital professional learning community. The role of the leader as culture builder carries new responsibilities that often read more like poetry than like a traditional job description:

- Creates sparks, marshals forces, tends fires, and celebrates victories.
- Believes in and releases the potential of followers.
- Unites dynamic and diverse communities for the good of the whole.

We acknowledge that many forms of leadership exist within schools. For the purpose of this conversation, the school leader is the *designated site-based leader*, such as the director, headmaster, or principal. We are also making several assumptions about leadership for building professional learning communities in schools:

- The leader lives by and models deeply held values and beliefs. Keshavan Nair (1994), in *Lessons from the Life of Gandhi*, concludes, "Leadership by example is not only the most pervasive but also the most enduring form of leadership" (p. 140). We assume that quality leaders "walk the talk" in every aspect of their work.
- The leader is well grounded in her sense of self. In *The Tao of Leadership*, John Heider (1985) states this assumption simply but

eloquently, "I know where I stand and I know what I stand for: that is ground" (p. 51). It is impossible to lead others in meaningful conversations about the future, about deeply held beliefs, about relationships, and about learning without self-understanding.

• Change efforts are more successful when they emanate from within the school community and are supported by its leader. Staff attitudes and actions about change, innovation, and professional learning are significantly influenced by the leader's disposition.

The following sections highlight the five critical qualities of leadership and their attendant actions.

Vision

In *Leading Without Power*, Max DePree (1997) draws a distinction between vision and sight: "We can teach ourselves to see things the way they are. Only with vision can we begin to see things the way they can be" (pp. 116–117). DePree is describing the future-focused quality of leadership that is essential in creating a meaningful context for action in learning communities. Future-focused leadership is the ability to look beyond the present circumstances and conjure an image of the future that recognizes and responds to the need for change. A community that has a future-focused culture talks about what's possible and what new opportunities are available, not what's wrong or what needs to be fixed (see box, "Case Study on Vision").

The school vision is not solely the brainchild of the school leader but is born out of a community's conversation regarding the question "What do we want to become?" School leaders share their image and invite all members of the school community to verbalize their hopes and dreams for the future of the children in their school. The conversation focuses on communicating ideas; listening to each other; and discovering, nurturing, and articulating a vision that is inspiring and compelling to everyone. Teachers whose hopes and dreams have dimmed as a result of their teaching experiences will need help in restoring their visions. Future-focused leaders work with disappointed teachers and help them rediscover their reason for entering the teaching profession.

A vision becomes the community's road map to the future: It connects dreams and aspirations, offers hope for a different future, and bonds diverse people and their perspectives. To sustain this communal energy and hope, the leader must hold the vision high for all to see, constantly revisit it, expand on it, and continuously help members of the community connect with it and find ways to personalize it and make it their own. The goal is to unite people through a mutually held vision and then support the people in changing the vision into a reality. Peter Senge (1990) says, "Leadership is ultimately about creating new realities." We agree. To us, a powerful leader inspires dreams, marshals the forces, and tends the fires until vision becomes reality.

Values

Let's play the word association game: You say a word and then I say the first word that comes into my mind. You say "leader" and I quickly say "values." The association of leader and values conjures a mental image of Gandhi dying in India with violence rising in the streets all

Case Study on Vision: Westlake Elementary School

Westlake Elementary School, with its 350 students and 22 staff members, is part of a large school district that serves 110,000 students. The school staff is characterized by an attitude of acceptance of all the children in the school. For several years, Westlake Elementary has successfully served its own student population with learning disabilities (LD), as well as the increasing number of students with limited English proficiency (LEP) who have joined the school community. In addition, during this school year, two students have become eligible for special education services for the emotionally disabled, and one student has been diagnosed as mildly mentally retarded. As this school year closes, the staff is preparing for the next one. They are anticipating that most of their kindergarten students with LEP will attend a special center at another school and that the students with disabilities will transfer to schools with appropriate disability programs.

At a school faculty meeting, a 1st grade teacher suggests that the students with LEP stay at Westlake, their own community school. The school speech and language pathologist offers to support the primary teachers in adapting curriculum for students with LEP. The principal (Ms. Gray), the LD teacher, and the 2nd and 3rd grade teachers are all interested in exploring ways in which they can serve the three students identified for special education in their classrooms so that these students can remain at Westlake

with their siblings. At a meeting, Ms. Gray asks her staff, "Are we ready to begin a journey to become an inclusive school in which all children are welcome and all children can learn?"

The speech and language pathologist comments that as the school's population becomes more diverse, staff want to learn more about new student groups and how to meet their needs. A 2nd grade teacher volunteers that she has enrolled in a minicourse on working with parents from other cultures.

Most of the staff agree that they would like to pursue the possibility of inviting these students to remain at Westlake and plan to create teams to further discuss their commitments to children and families.

Many of the staff also express a common commitment to the children and families they serve. As the discussion progresses, several additional staff become interested in other possibilities and express a willingness to explore and learn together. Ms. Gray is creating opportunities for her staff to begin a journey toward a vision.

✔ This case study demonstrates that leaders can share with their teaching staff an image of the future that is different from the current reality and is respectful of their beliefs, needs, and interests. The staff will become engaged in further defining their vision and committed to learning processes to create a new reality.

around. He hasn't had anything to eat or drink for many days, and his life systems are slowly shutting down. He refuses to eat or drink until all the people in his country demonstrate that they are committed to the value of nonviolence.

Gandhi's fast is an expression of his commitment to the values of nonviolence. His "way of being" teaches a poignant lesson: Leaders, by their words and actions, are the keepers of values. Such words and actions emanate from deep within the heart of the leader. From this base of "knowing thyself," the leader is able to begin the work of calling forth the values and beliefs of the members of the organization. For example, the principal helps the members of the school community unveil their common values and define what they stand for and value as a collective. Articulating these values provides a beginning point for bonding among members of the school community. The values become the moral and ethical foundation for the work of the leader and the organization and guide them in decision making.

The next challenge of leadership is making visible these mutually held values and beliefs. Harvey and Lucia (1997), in *144 Ways to Walk the Talk*, advise that "the true purpose of our values statements is to guide both our behaviors and our decisions" (p. 7). The role of the leader is to ensure that values are transformed into action. The leader conscientiously monitors the fidelity between values and actions.

Many school communities have labored to develop a school mission statement and articulate their values and beliefs about teaching and learning. Yet staff often do not reference these statements when they design their instructional programs. Nair (1994), in *Lessons Learned from Gandhi*, says, "If we don't

operationalize our ideals, they are often nothing more than slogans" (p. 26). The leader asks community members to commit to their ideals and then strive to align their actions with these ideals. People will make mistakes and miss their goals, but "knowing we will not be able to attain perfection is no excuse for not making a commitment" (Nair, p. 26). A quality leader offers the community the courage to speak its convictions, the strength to live by them, and the opportunities to operationalize them (see box, "Case Study on Values").

Service

Just as "ethical" and "moral" are words associated with values-based leadership, "steward" and "servant" are associated with service-based leadership. A service-based leader acts as a steward to the purpose, vision, and values of the organization and to its individual members. According to Peter Block (1993), stewardship is the willingness to be accountable for the well-being of the larger organization by operating in service, rather than in control, of those around us. Stewardship is different from charismatic leadership in that the light does not shine solely on the power of the leader but rather on the community members and their contributions. In *The Tao of Leadership*, Heider (1985) offers a simple image to illustrate service-based leadership:

> Imagine you are a midwife, you are assisting someone else's birth. Do good without showing fuss. Facilitate what is happening rather than what you think ought to be happening. If you must take the lead, lead so that the mother is helped, yet still free and in charge.

When the baby is born, the mother will rightly say, "We did it ourselves!" (p. 33).

Thomas Sergiovanni (1996) describes service leadership in schools as "a commitment to administer to the needs of the school as an institution by serving its purposes, by serving those who struggle to embody these purposes, and by acting as a guardian to protect the institutional integrity of the school" (p. 88). In schools, principals operationalize this idea by establishing infrastructures that "clear the way" for staff to realize their full potential and advance the vision of the school. The school principal clears the way by providing needed resources, planning for ongoing collaboration, eliminating impeding practices, enrolling the public in the work of the school, and protecting the integrity of the school.

For example, if the school is not producing the desired results, the principal challenges the staff to revisit what they are doing; and when difficult issues arise, the staff confront and negotiate the issues, not ignore them. In *Total Leaders* (1998), Charles Schwahn and William

Case Study on Values: Sanford Elementary School

Because his previous experiences in the school system demonstrate a strong belief system and well-articulated commitment to inclusion, Dr. Beamer was chosen for the principalship of Sanford Elementary School.

Twenty years ago, as a classroom teacher, Dr. Beamer initiated a relationship with the special education and the LEP teachers who were serving his students. He invited them to coteach with him and regularly used his lunch break to plan with them. He encouraged his students to identify and speak openly about their uniqueness. Dr. Beamer modeled for his students an appreciation of each of their differences. In a staff development position, Dr. Beamer facilitated teacher research projects on the teacher's role in developing an inclusive classroom community. These projects provided teachers with an opportunity to reflect on their own biases, prejudices, and present practices, and then create new or different practices to further inclusive classroom communities. Before Sanford Elementary School opened its doors, Dr. Beamer was able to select and then meet with its future faculty. Together they explored such questions as "How will we welcome and honor all members of our school community?" and "How will we work together to ensure that all share in the responsibility of educating our children?"

✔ This case study demonstrates that Dr. Beamer is an educator who consistently "leads from the heart" and from a set of values about respecting and including everyone. His actions throughout his career speak to a passion about his belief system. In his positions of leadership, he has created opportunities for discussion, has shared decision making, and has honored each person's contribution to the community.

Spady elaborate on the challenge and responsibility of service leadership:

> While the term service sounds soft, the duty is hard. When obstacles are impeding success . . . [the leaders] insist changes be made. When the integrity of the organization's purpose and success are at stake, they are the first to step up (p. 104).

Service-based leadership is especially applicable to a school where a culture of collaborating, learning, and innovating predominates among the staff. In a collaborative environment, the school leader serves the community as a guide, not as a controlling force. The leader who is in service holds the vision and the expectations of the community high enough for all to see and then supports and empowers the school's staff to continuously develop the knowledge, skills, and strategies necessary to realize the school's vision (see box, "Case Study on Service").

A leader who serves also allows the staff to make key decisions about their work with children. When initiatives come along, staff are allotted time to study them, talk about them, experiment with them in the classroom, and reflect on their efficacy. Staff are expected to evaluate both new and old practices in relationship to the school's values and purpose and their desired outcomes for students. When staff have the freedom to explore, experiment, find new resources, and try new practices, they begin organizing themselves into groups for support and reflection. Within these groups, members assume leadership roles. Before long, multiple leaders emerge, thus strengthening the school's capacity to realize its goals.

Capacity Building

> Vital organizations have adopted an attitude of lifetime learning, and they help their members make everyday learning a reality in their lives. The nourishment of individuals lies at the heart of vital organizations, and the nourishment of individuals begins with the opportunity to learn (DePree, 1997, p. 105).

A school cannot realize its vision without expanding the skill and knowledge base of its staff. Through capacity-building activities, a school begins to close the gap between its current abilities and needed capabilities—for both individuals and the school as a whole.

At the individual level, a quality leader ignites and nurtures each person's capacity to learn, grow, and change. A climate that encourages risk taking is fundamental when staff members need to stretch beyond what they know and explore frontiers. DePree (1997) feels that risk taking offers "opportunities to move closer to our potential. Risks result in a kind of learning available in no other way" (pp. 144–145). In an organization that prizes learning, risks cease to be threatening, and people can learn powerful lessons from success and failure. Sometimes our most poignant learning comes from failed attempts.

In this risk-taking environment, the leader often acts as a coach who helps clarify goals and encourages action. For some, encouragement means stimulating new ways of thinking; for others, it means shoring up self-confidence. Regardless of the approach, the coach ultimately retreats, letting the learners spread their wings and take their bows.

The effect of individual capacity building

Case Study on Service: Lakeside Elementary School

Lakeside Elementary School has five pods, each with six classrooms and a shared common area. The school staff have organized themselves into family groupings—that is, groupings that include multiple grade levels. Such groupings ensure continuity of instruction across grade levels and increased opportunities for multi-age groupings, integration, and relationships between students and teachers.

Each "family-cluster" teaching team meets bimonthly. Either the principal, Ms. Roley, or assistant principal, Mr. DelRosa, attends one monthly meeting per team and addresses questions, concerns, or challenges about instruction and collaboration. Family meetings are primarily focused on team planning and instructional issues. Most administrative matters are handled by memo or at the quarterly faculty meetings.

Feedback from these self-organized teams has led the staff and administration to agree on several significant schoolwide changes: (1) parent meetings are now conducted according to family group instead of grade level; (2) monthly parent meetings are scheduled alternately during the evening and daytime hours; (3) a position for a "multiple intelligences" resource teacher has been created; and (4) all teachers have the option of making two home visits per year.

Lakeside Elementary is an example of a school whose infrastructure is consistent with the vision, values, and purpose of the school community: The family groupings and staff cluster meetings promote a continuity of instruction and relationships among staff, students, and families. A master schedule permits joint planning time that facilitates ongoing collaboration, learning, and capacity building.

✔ This case study demonstrates that the decisions of the leadership of Lakeside Elementary are driven by the vision of the school and by a high regard for serving the faculty. The leader is attentive to the recommendations of the learning teams and family clusters; teachers are empowered to create a school that is constantly moving in the direction of fulfilling their vision.

within a school is exponential because it enables an entire school community to become more competent as it journeys toward its vision. But developing the "collective mind" cannot be left to chance. Faculty members require time and opportunities to learn and reflect on quality practices together. Leaders must consider ways to facilitate the ongoing questions of (1) how to encourage school-based study groups and (2) how to align emerging practices with the school vision. Leaders create expectations for high levels of individual and organizational competence when they incorporate physical and temporal infrastructures within a school that promotes ongoing collaboration among professionals for sharing information, knowledge, and skills (see box, "Case Study on Capacity Building").

Case Study on Capacity Building: Oakwood Elementary School

The faculty, parents, and administration of Oakwood Elementary School have developed a vision for their school: All students receive an individualized, high-quality education program that recognizes their unique characteristics and maximizes their potential in both the academic and personal-social domains. Parents and faculty have agreed to institute two multi-age classes at every grade level in two years.

To help build the staff's capacity to realize this vision, the principal has both surveyed and interviewed staff members about their needs and interests. After reviewing staff surveys and current research about professional development and school change, the principal has reallocated funds to support three major thrusts for staff development during the school year: (1) on- and off-site observations and debriefings, (2) teacher research groups on topics identified by staff, and (3) acquisition of resources on multi-age and related topics for the school's professional library.

✔ In this case study, the principal recognizes that for change and improvement to occur, the knowledge, skills, and strategies of the staff need to be developed and enriched. The principal also respects the ability of the faculty members to identify professional development goals that will improve both their individual and the school's capacity to create a different future.

Relationship Building

Recently, while discussing teaming and collaborating, the staff of an elementary school generated a list of successful teams: the Chicago Bulls, Seinfeld Company, and Roy Rogers and Dale Evans. Several staffers quickly decided that a supertalented leader, such as TV star Jerry Seinfeld or basketball hero Michael Jordan, was the cause of the team's success. This is the image of the leader as the hero whose charisma motivates all. An alternative image of leadership is emerging: the leader as an architect of relationships. In this capacity, the leader designs a workplace where relationships are primary, where a sense of belonging and trust is pervasive, where diversity is valued, and where connections are open and active.

Creating an atmosphere of belonging—a feeling of connectedness—is a primary role of the leader. Abraham Maslow's (1954) hierarchy of needs suggests that a sense of belonging and acceptance precedes our ability to perform to our potential. When we are in relationships with others, we learn more about ourselves and our individual and collective potential. Belonging creates a climate of safety where risk taking for the purpose of capacity building can thrive. The leader sets the tone for belonging.

Relationships are also based on trust. Stephen Covey (1990), in *Principle-Centered Leadership,* offers some insights into the leader's role in developing a trusting organization. Covey believes that trust between people emerges from a core of trustworthiness. Trustworthiness is a personal phenomenon that combines character and competence. Leaders demonstrate trustworthiness through their personal integrity and professional competence while they simultaneously create opportunities for staff to demonstrate their trustworthiness. The combination of these actions supports the development of group trust.

The leader as architect of relationships values diversity. Leaders who truly value diversity are challenged by different thinking and work styles and capitalize on the potential of congregating groups with diverse perspectives. Leaders intentionally move in different circles and seek ideas at the periphery. In building professional learning communities in schools, the principal who values diversity promotes multidisciplinary representation on collaborative learning teams and provides opportunities for learning teams to seek new or different perspectives.

Leaders in vital organizations seek new ways to connect people to each other. Margaret Wheatley and Myron Kellner-Rogers (1996) advise that (1) the more access people have to one another, the more possibilities there are and (2) when structured organizational charts thwart access to people and information, individual and organizational potential is diminished. People need to be free to reach anywhere to accomplish their work. Leaders are responsible for creating the structures, both human and technological, that give an organization access to itself and the larger world.

Relationships are central to developing professional learning communities. Leaders who weave strong, dynamic webs of relationships in their schools help build the trust and the stimulation necessary to step into the world of innovation (see box, "Case Study on Relationship Building").

❧   ❧   ❧

This chapter has isolated five qualities of leadership that are central to building professional learning communities in our schools. Yet in reality, the school leader does not wear one hat at a time but rather juggles multiple roles. In *A New Vision for Staff Development*, Rosie O'Brian Votjek, an elementary school principal, describes her experience as a leader of a future-focused school:

> I served as a facilitator, consultant, instructor, and colleague who assisted teachers in integrating curriculum, using new instructional practices. . . . I promoted different kinds of staff development, but the most important thing I did was "walk the talk." I facilitated learning . . . [by] asking tough questions; managing the change process; serving as a cheerleader, supporter, and advocate for teachers; keeping the vision out front; helping to connect people. To do this, it is critical to get to know the teachers on an individual basis, to know their needs, and to celebrate their successes (Sparks & Hirsh, 1997, p. 100).

Leadership is best described as amorphous, complex, and ever changing. Leading the development of learning communities adds another level of ambiguity. Rebecca van der Bogert (1998), in *Making Learning Communities Work*, points out:

> The term *community of learners* is currently about as common and revered as motherhood and apple pie.

Case Study on Relationship Building: Crossroads Elementary School

Ms. Stevens is in her second year of leadership at Crossroads Elementary, a school with 785 students in preschool through 5th grade and 42 teachers. Ms. Stevens decided that this year she would abandon her monthly full faculty meetings to meet with the staff in small groups. Ms. Stevens' goals are to establish a better understanding of the needs of the staff, appreciate their gifts, and develop a plan to share the expertise of each with the others. Ms. Stevens now meets once a month with each team—early childhood and elementary. She has also worked out a rotation so that once every three weeks she meets individually with each member of the staff for 20 minutes. An end-of-the-year survey of the teaching staff indicates that as a team the members feel more closely connected, they use each other's expertise as resources more frequently than in the past, and they feel empowered by the support and understanding between the staff and the principal.

✔ As a result of Ms. Stevens' commitment to creating networks of relationships, the staff has become more knowledgeable. Establishing infrastructures that facilitate relationships has resulted in the staff's sense of empowerment.

Bringing the concept to reality is far more difficult than baking an apple pie, [although] the need for ongoing nurturance and the degree of challenge are perhaps comparable to motherhood (p. 71).

Transforming our schools into professional learning communities demands quality leadership—leadership that is a commitment of the heart, mind, and spirit; leadership that is about the future; and leadership where intention becomes reality.

Process

Part II offers practical guidance and tools for developing school-based professional learning communities. Chapter 4, "Identity of the Learning Community," provides a framework that supports a school community in discovering and articulating its identity. A natural alignment occurs within a community when its members have a clear sense of who they are collectively and where they are going. This chapter presents a rationale and strategies for exploring the many dimensions of a school community's identity, including its history, core purpose and values, current reality, and shared vision.

Chapter 5, "Learning as a Community," introduces the collaborative learning process—a process that supports staff and families in learning together. This chapter offers guidance on how to identify topics of study and form collaborative learning groups. Here, we present stages of the collaborative learning process, along with key questions, supporting activities, and examples.

Chapter 6, "Enhancing Capacity to Learn," highlights the interpersonal side of collaborative learning; discusses the kinds of group behavior that help build a bond of trust, belonging, and purposefulness; and focuses on tools and techniques that support group members in communicating and working effectively with each other.

Identity of the Learning Community

This chapter presents a framework that supports a school community in discovering its identity. A school community can only begin to know itself if the members explore their history, values, purpose, current reality, and vision. We can use many approaches to explore our school's identity. This chapter suggests activities that can help a community identify where it has been, where it is, and where it wants to go.

Teachers have long functioned in isolated classrooms, void of meaningful connections with colleagues. For those who seek to make connections and nurture others in this profession, isolation is both unwanted and unnatural. A new metaphor for schools is emerging—schools as communities—which is the opposite of the isolated, compartmentalized approach to education. At the heart of the concept of community is wholeness and connectedness. Community is grounded in networks of relationships and a sense of identity.

If schools are to function as communities, many changes must occur.

First, individuals in a community need a clear sense of personal identity. Thoughtful reflection about self-identity prepares people to work in changing environments by helping them recognize and "own" their thoughts, emotions, hopes, and dreams.

Second, members of the school community must actively engage in discovering who they are as a community and what they want to create. Community members might include teaching staff, parents, administrators, students, support staff, and other community representatives. As this group engages in ongoing dialogue about its history, values, current situation, and dreams, a shared identity emerges. A good way to begin creating a shared identity is by becoming better acquainted.

Getting Acquainted

In every culture, social rules govern behavior when individuals meet strangers. There are greetings and polite ways to learn more about another person. In the United States, people often shake hands and say "hello" as a simple formality to start a conversation. When people form a group for learning together, they must first become acquainted. This process of getting acquainted sets the tone for future interactions. Within groups, people are often asked to introduce themselves—to state their names and to reveal other information about themselves. The following three activities offer group members an opportunity to get acquainted.

What's in It for Me? Participants walk around the room, introduce themselves, and share what they hope to learn from the meeting. This activity both warms up the room and focuses participants on their expectations for the event.

Designer Name Tags. Participants decorate their name tags with pictures, words, or phrases that reveal something about themselves. They form groups of three and introduce themselves. Groups change every few minutes.

Polaroid Pictures. As participants enter the event, the facilitator takes their picture and asks them to write their name and three things about themselves on a label. The participants then attach their pictures and personal information labels to a poster board, creating a permanent display of the community. This activity requires a Polaroid camera, film, adhesive labels, marking pens, and a large poster board.

Sharing Perspectives

Learning together is an interactive process that requires not only getting acquainted, but also continually learning about each other's perspectives. Additional "getting acquainted" activities continue to uncover the diversity of values, beliefs, and experiences within a group. The following activities offer participants opportunities to share their unique perspectives and learn about their colleagues:

True Confessions in Four Corners (Carter & Curtis, 1994). The facilitator prepares the room with the paraphernalia (a poster or a prop) for different roles (e.g., ship's captain, medic, guardian angel, or tour guide) displayed in each corner. The facilitator asks participants to move to the corner that best describes them as a teacher. Once participants gather in the corner with other colleagues, they discuss the reasons for their choice. They then share this information with participants in the other corners. The facilitator may ask questions such as "Did members in your group have different reasons for choosing the same corner?" or "What surprised you about the explanations given by the groups in the other corners?" Such an activity reveals participants' beliefs about their role and demonstrates that different people may interpret the same role differently. For example, to some people, a tour guide plans wonderful trips in coordination with the wishes of the client. To others, a tour guide dictates the itinerary without considering the client.

The Job Game (Carter & Curtis, 1994). The facilitator creates index cards with roles on them, such as gardener, artist, lawyer, plumber, and banker. The facilitator puts the cards on tables, and participants circulate and collect cards until they have several cards they want to keep. In small groups, participants share their reasons for their card selections. Group members can explore the following questions: (1) "What appeals to you about the jobs/roles you kept?" (2) "Does this role capitalize on something you are good at?" (3) "Is this role completely different from your current job, or is it related?" An alternative way to play this game is to give each person two to three cards and ask people to trade cards until they get the ones they like. The conversation is lively during the trading process as participants try to collect the roles they value.

Your Calling. The facilitator asks participants to draw a picture, make a collage, or create a graphic that captures their memory of what "called" them to the teaching profession. Ask them to think about what they were hoping and dreaming when they decided to become teachers. Using paper, markers, and crayons, everyone takes approximately 15 minutes to represent their thoughts. Participants share pictures and stories in small groups. Each person gets 5 minutes of uninterrupted time to talk about his calling. This sharing is followed by group discussion during which participants are encouraged to ask each other questions. This activity offers each participant an opportunity to recall memorable points in time, special people, and significant events that affected her career choice.

Moments of Magic. This activity provides a method for sharing personal/professional histories with colleagues. The facilitator hangs a "Moments of Magic" chart (see Figure 4.1) in a school hallway or teacher's lunchroom. Marking pens are attached to the chart. Staff members fill in their squares by a certain date. Staff then use the chart to learn more about each other and to "tease out" magical things about their team.

Exploring Our History

Exploring the history of a school community answers the question "Where have we been?" We study and reflect on past events both to learn from the past and to develop a better understanding of our current situation. Often sources of inspiration, the school's stories tell the tales of achievement and disappointment, of pride and sorrow.

A variety of methods provides glimpses of the history of a school community: a scrapbook, a slide show, a "memorable moments" collage, or retrospective talks from veteran staff and community members. "Histomapping" (Bailey, 1995), a whole-group method for exploring the history of an organization, allows groups of people to visually represent important events in the life of their community on a time line. As each member of the group adds pictures or symbols to a Histomap, a common base of information about the past is generated. The group honors the experiences and wisdom of veteran members, while novice members have an opportunity to more fully understand

FIGURE 4.1 Moments of Magic Chart					
Community Member	**Sue**	**Mark**	**Brenda**	**Natalie**	**Lisa**
Magical Motivator: belief or issue about which you are passionate					
Magical People: persons who have strongly influenced you professionally					
Magical Events: experiences that have shaped you professionally					

the historical forces that had an effect on the school. By honoring the past and reaping its wisdom, the group as a whole is better positioned to explore the future.

Using the "Histomap," educators may explore a variety of historical themes or categories (see Figure 4.2). In the example in Figure 4.2, a group of principals in a school district identified significant events in 10-year increments in the categories of (1) curriculum, (2) delivery of services, (3) children and families, and (4) leadership. The Histomap process helped to identify trends that had occurred in the district.

Categories on the Histomap vary with the group. Other Histomap categories might include policies, facilities, communities, and key people. The time span explored also varies with the group. Suzanne Bailey (1995) suggests that when creating a Histomap, a school should look as far into the past as it wants to look into the future. For example, if a school wants to plan 10 years into its future, staff need to examine at least the past 10 years of events in the school.

Once staff members have attached all the pictures or symbols to the Histomap and have shared the stories behind the pictures, the group examines the entire spectrum of significant events. Here are questions the group might explore:

• What lessons can we learn from the past?
• Do we have different interpretations of the same event?
• Are there recurring patterns or emerging trends?
• What are the specific strengths and weaknesses of our community?

By discussing these questions, the group

may establish shared meaning and a common background of knowledge. Having the whole group construct and interpret the history of its community is a significant step in establishing a group identity.

Articulating Our Core Ideology

"Core ideology defines the enduring character of an organization [and in times of change] . . . provides the glue that holds an organization together" (Collins & Porras, 1996, p. 66). The core ideology of a school community is its core purpose and core values. Successful schools incorporate their core ideology into their daily workings. In these schools, the core ideology is more than a mission statement that hangs on the wall—it is a force that permeates the building and is perpetuated by those within the school community.

The diversity of the people within a school gives rise to different perspectives about the core ideology. Individuals bring a set of personal beliefs and values that have been shaped over the years. Articulating a core ideology, therefore, necessitates finding the common ground among diverse views. Common ground is different from consensus in that it involves forming alignment rather than agreement. Finding common ground both acknowledges the value in different perspectives and looks for commonalities among such perspectives. During this process of finding common ground, we need to hear and appreciate differences, rather than attempt to reconcile them. We are not being asked to surrender our perspectives. Rather, we are asked to listen for our perspectives in the voices of others. By making concerted efforts to unearth the common ground

FIGURE 4.2
Histomap

Before 1970	1970	1980	1990

Curriculum

Spelling   Social Studies   Integrated curriculum
Reading   Science   Thematic-based instruction
Math

                           Whole language

Basal Reader   Language   Novel-based units   Reading and
                           experience   grouped by ability level   writing connection

Delivery of Services

4th	5th	6th	Other
			ED
1st grade	2nd grade	3rd grade	MR
			LD

Separate

4	5th	Special education
K–1	2–3	

Multiage

4, 5, 6, Special ed
1, 2, 3, Special ed

Integrated and combined

Children and Families

Mom, Dad, kids

Grandma, Aunt Sue, kids

Leadership

Teacher as Leader

Teacher as Leader

Note: Abbreviations for certain disabilities: ED = emotional disturbance; LD = learning disabilities; MR = mild retardation.

existing within our school community, we strengthen the bonds of established relationships while we create new relationships.

Core Purpose

The core purpose of a school community is the component of core ideology that answers the question "Why do we exist?" The core purpose is different from a school's goals in that the core purpose cannot be fulfilled. "It is like a guiding star on the horizon—forever pursued but never reached" (Collins & Porras, 1996, p. 69). The core purpose captures the idealism of the organization. It is the work of every school community to discover its unique purpose—a purpose that reflects its ideals, its soul, its essence.

Here are two examples of a school's core purpose:

• At Middletown Elementary School, we will create and nurture a community of lifelong learners.

• At Essex Elementary School, we will work together to effectively meet the needs of all our students and families.

Collins and Porras (1996) have suggested three methods to help a group articulate its core purpose.

Method 1. Begin at the individual level by asking each group member to reflect on the following two questions: (1) "Why did you choose to belong to this community or this profession?" and (2) "What deeper sense of purpose motivates you to dedicate your time and energy each day to this work?" Individuals share their thoughts with the group and look for a common bond.

Method 2. In this activity the group asks "Why?" five times. The group begins with a descriptive statement of what they do. For example:

• "We do X." Then they ask, "Why is that important?" for five times.

• "We educate children." Why is that important?

• "So they can be productive citizens." Why is that important?

• By the fifth "Why is that important?" the essence of why we are together begins to be voiced.

Method 3. In this activity, the group discusses the question "What would happen if our program, our school, or our service ceased to exist?" This question helps a group get in touch with why it exists.

When first articulating the core purpose, the group should not get stuck in finding the perfect phrases. Discovering the heart and soul of the organization, its "reason for being," takes time. The initial document is a working document that will be revisited and revised many times throughout the process of creating a school's identity.

Core Values

A core value is a central belief deeply understood and shared by every member of an organization. Core values guide the actions of everyone in the organization; they focus its energy and are the anchor points for all its plans (Saphier & D'Auria, 1993, p. 3).

The core values of a school community form its belief system. A powerful message is available to the students and families in the school when an entire staff is operating from the same set of values. For example, a school that believes that "all children learn and all children belong" has strong pillars to guide its actions. With a core of shared values, the staff can act autonomously, yet harmony is in the message that permeates the school.

Communities typically have only a few core values that are meaningful to everyone. In identifying core values, seeking common ground, rather than consensus, is important. To force consensus about deeply felt beliefs would be incompatible with the concept of core values. The following are examples of a school's core values:

- We believe learning is an ongoing, individualized process.
- We believe all people learn.
- We respect and value individual differences.

Core values depict a way of being. They describe the essential nature of an organization. Two questions help to distinguish values that have enduring qualities from values that are based on current trends:

- Which values do we envision being valid for our community in 100 years?
- Would we lose a significant piece of our identity as a school if this value was absent?

Because values are the underlying, constant force that guides practice, they must be distinguished from practice. Values are not subject to change, whereas practice may change over time. For example, a core value mentioned previously is that we believe learning is an ongoing, individualized process. In the 1970s, the practice most commonly associated with that value was the pullout model of service delivery.

If children needed gifted or special education, they most often received specialized instruction in a separate room with a specialist. Today, a more common practice is an integrated model of service delivery in which teachers and specialists provide the specialized instruction in the general education classroom. The core value that learning is an ongoing, individualized process is the same in both situations. The best practice has changed.

We can often find discrepancies in what we say we believe and what we practice on a daily basis. For example, if a school community holds a belief that children are first, does this belief permeate the school environment? Are teachers willing to do whatever it takes to put children first? Do children's needs and interests drive school decisions? Do parents feel that their children are the top priority of the school? Articulating values is often easier than incorporating them into daily practice. A school community must have tools to examine both discrepancies and alignment between values and actions.

Schools have many arenas, such as the daily classroom routine, the instructional materials, the evaluation system, the discipline procedures, the lunchroom, or the teachers' workroom, where core values are evident (Saphier & D'Auria, 1993). In a school where practice is congruent with core values, the values would be evident in every arena. The daily routine, the discipline procedure, and the organization of the teachers' workroom would support learning as an ongoing, individualized process. Examining current practice in light of the school's core values, one arena at a time, provides a conduit for aligning a school community with its belief system.

Assessing Current Reality

Many forces affect a school's current reality. These forces, emerging from both inside and outside the school building, include students and their families, staff expertise and diversity, organizational structure, human and fiscal resources, school initiatives, and school climate.

Each individual in a school community perceives the effect of these forces differently—and perceptions of the same force may be either positive or negative. One example is the effect of an increasingly diverse population within the school community. Some staff may find additional languages and cultures to be an overwhelming burden, whereas others may view this addition as an opportunity to create a culturally rich learning environment.

Understanding the forces affecting a community is an important part of looking toward the future. Often, dreams appear unattainable because of present forces or obligations. Assessing current reality provides a forum for viewing how things actually are in relation to how we would like them to be. Questions guiding this process might be "What are we doing?" or "Are our practices getting us what we want?"

Teams might use several other tools to examine current reality:

Context Mapping (The Grove Consultants International, 1997).* This tool offers participants a visual representation of the significant external forces affecting a school's current

---

*Adapted by permission of The Grove Consultants International, P.O. Box 29391, 1000 Torney Ave., San Francisco, CA 94129-0391; phones: 1-800-494-7683; 1-415-561-2500; World Wide Web: http://www.grove. com

situation (see Figure 4.3). To begin this activity, hang a 4' x 6' piece of chart paper on a wall. Draw a big picture of the school in the middle. Participants write the positive and negative external elements that affect school functioning on Post-it notes, one element per Post-it. Participants pick two to three elements they feel are most important and share them with the group. Cluster the ideas together and label their categories. Then arrange the categories on the chart in a way that best depicts the impact of the external environment on the school community.

Current Snapshot (Bailey, 1995). This activity identifies the current initiatives in a school and the degree to which they have been implemented. In "Current Snapshot" (see Figure 4.4 on p. 41), participants list all the initiatives, projects, and programs with which their school is currently involved. Then participants discuss the status of each program (whether it is in a start-up phase, a full-implementation stage, or a stagnant stage). Together, participants place each program on the appropriate area of a "tree" image or poster: seeds, buds, full flowers, withering flowers, or compost pile. The group then uses this visual image of the school's initiatives, projects, and programs for strategic planning and priority setting.

The Force Field Analysis. This activity, Tool 1 in Part III, "Tools for Learning," can help teams assess a school's current reality. Here, group members brainstorm ways to enhance "facilitating" forces and ways to meet the challenges of "constraining" forces.

Each of these tools provides useful visual diagrams that help a school community develop a common understanding of the forces currently affecting its development.

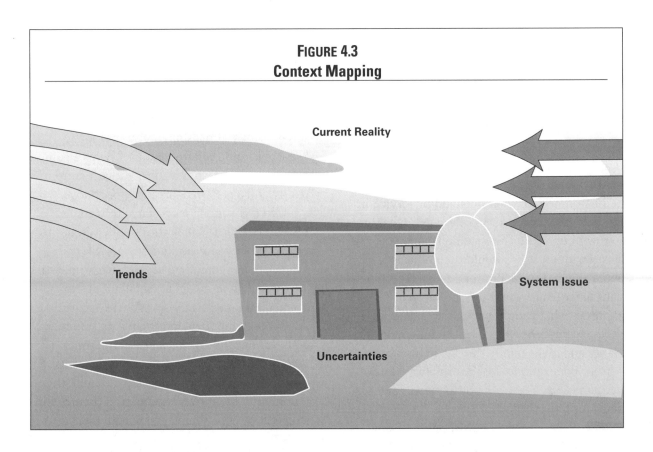

FIGURE 4.3
Context Mapping

Creating a Shared Vision

A shared vision is a clear, compelling image of the community's future. It answers the question "What do we want to create?" A shared vision is aligned with the core purpose of the community, but it is more specific. The core purpose states a general direction for the community, such as "Go west!" while the shared vision describes the specific destination—"to the top of that mountain." A shared vision inspires members of the community because it enfolds the dreams of each individual into a community dream. This dream is formulated into a statement that clearly articulates the school's commitment to the education of its children.

An example of a shared vision statement is "Our school is a playground for learning." From this big-picture statement, it is helpful to create minipictures, or statements, of specific, measurable results. Minipictures are formed by considering questions like these:

- How do we know when we have reached our vision?
- What will our children be doing?
- What will our teachers be doing? Our administrators? Our parents?

The answers to these questions "ground" the vision in reality and provide benchmarks for tracking progress.

Creating a shared vision begins when we

voice our personal visions—What do we, as individuals, want to accomplish in our life and in our work? The following activities help educators begin to identify their personal/professional visions.

Awards Banquet. The facilitator asks participants to imagine an awards banquet being held 10 years in the future where they are being honored for their outstanding service in the field of education. A colleague is speaking to the group about the accomplishments of the award winner. What would their colleague say about them? The facilitator asks each participant to write a two-minute speech that expresses what they hope will be said about their accomplishments. This exercise helps clarify and make public the dream inside each person. For example, Ms. Smith always knew her purpose as a teacher was to prepare her students for future academic success. Through the Awards Banquet exercise, Ms. Smith discovered that she was passionate about instilling a love of learning in each of her students. She will know she has accomplished this when her students are consistently inquisitive, motivated, and excited about their work.

Making a Difference (Saphier & D'Auria, 1993). Here is another question that helps clarify the vision of teaching staff: "In what ways do you want your students to be different as a result of having spent this year with you?" After reflecting on this question, staff share answers and document their hopes and dreams on a large chart. The public expression of each community member's personal aspirations provides the school community with an authentic base on which to create a shared vision.

After talking about personal visions and desires, a community is ready to begin formu-

lating its shared vision of the community's future. Part III, "Tools for Learning," includes several activities to help a community develop its shared vision. Tools 3 and 4, "Affinity" and "Open Space," facilitate the merging of personal visions into a shared vision. Tool 2, "Probable and Preferred Future," helps a community look at trends associated with current reality and a preferred direction for change.

Often the group is too large to work as a unit and needs to break into smaller groups to begin the shared-visioning process. Skits, songs, poems, commercials, and magazine articles are all great media for small groups to voice their collective vision for the future. After the groups develop their skits, commercials, or magazine articles, the community reconvenes; and each small group shares its vision. When all the groups have shared, the community identifies the common themes and shapes a "rough" shared vision statement.

Vision Commercial. Participants develop a commercial that markets the group's vision. The commercial is a 10-second spot that sells the vision. The following are tips to help create the commercial:

• Think in terms of sounds and visual images that capture your future.
• Think of three images that blend together in a 10-second spot:
First Image → Second Image → Third Image →
• Think of a caption or sound bite for each image.
• Draw, describe, or act out your commercial.

Magazine Cover Story (The Grove Consultants International, 1997). Participants

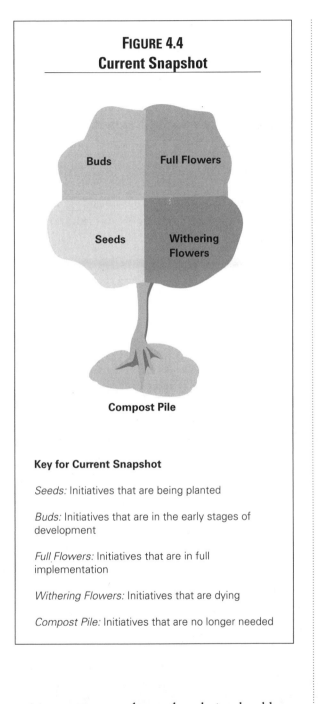

FIGURE 4.4
Current Snapshot

Buds

Full Flowers

Seeds

Withering
Flowers

Compost Pile

Key for Current Snapshot

Seeds: Initiatives that are being planted

Buds: Initiatives that are in the early stages of development

Full Flowers: Initiatives that are in full implementation

Withering Flowers: Initiatives that are dying

Compost Pile: Initiatives that are no longer needed

write a cover story about what their school has accomplished 10 years from now. The following suggested elements can be included in the cover story:

- Bigger-than-life headline.
- Bulleted list of outstanding accomplishments.
- Pictures that support accomplishments.
- Actions we took to get were we are.

Creating a vital shared vision is a lengthy process that requires multiple opportunities for active conversation followed by reflection. The community continually revisits its shared vision statement to refine and ensure its meaningfulness. Collins and Porras (1996) offer advice on creating an inspirational shared vision:

> There are no right answers. Did Beethoven create the right Ninth Symphony? Did Shakespeare create the right Hamlet? We can't answer these questions. . . . The envisioned future involves essential questions. Does this vision get your juices flowing? Do we find it stimulating? Does it spur forward momentum? (p. 75).

☛   ☛   ☛

Discovering an identity as a school community is a multiphase, multilayer process that requires the community to delve deep into its heart and soul. The community may not be proud of its past or may be discouraged by its current reality. The process of discovering a shared identity involves owning up to and accepting feelings about both personal identity and the identity of the school. This process can create an emotionally volatile atmosphere within the school. A roller-coaster ride is a metaphor people commonly use to describe the feelings we may experience when digging through the past, examining the present realities, and creating a new future. On a roller coaster, we tend to rise up high on the tracks as we envision and articulate our ideal future and then rapidly drop into dismay as we examine our day-to-day constraints. As we begin to see new possibilities in our current reality, the mood lightens again. This up-and-down ride continues through the various stages of the change process as we seek to learn more about who we are as a school and what we want to become (see Figure 4.5).

In school communities, everyone has a voice in creating the future. Collective conversations about the school community's history, values, purpose, current reality, and vision support the creation of a shared identity and serve as a conduit for forming deep and meaningful relationships within the school. The search for identity—who we are and who we want to be—is a vehicle for us to collectively and continuously renew our school community and discover better ways to educate our children.

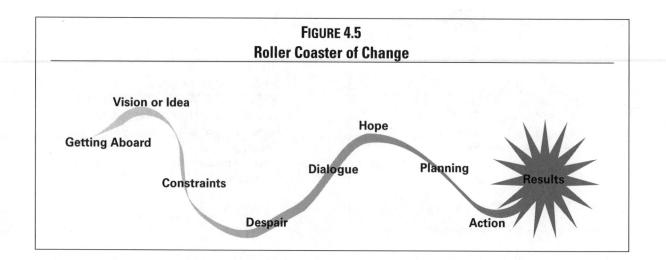

FIGURE 4.5
Roller Coaster of Change

Learning as a Community

As professionals in the field of education, many of us have mastered the skill of learning individually, but our capacity to learn collectively is underdeveloped. This chapter introduces a process that supports staff in learning together—a process that helps develop collaborative cultures— "where people continually expand their capacity to create the results they truly desire, where new and expansive patterns of thinking are nurtured, and where collective aspiration is set free" (Senge, 1990, p. 3). The *collaborative learning process* begins as people discover and express their personal aspirations and needs. Collaborative learning teams then form around shared interests. The teams explore, talk about, and experiment with many ideas. Finally, new practices emerge. We have woven a scenario involving Hayward Elementary School throughout the chapter to illustrate the application of the collaborative learning process.

Establishing a Staff Development Plan

We expect teachers to give their all to the growth and development of students. But a teacher cannot sustain such giving unless the conditions exist for the continued growth and

development of the teacher (Sarason, 1993, p. 62).

The previous chapter, "Identity of the Learning Community," presents ways that a school community can explore its identity and create its vision. When creating a vision, the staff decide what the school will look like at a future point in time and then develop specific, measurable outcomes associated with that vision. The process of exploring identity and sharing visions leaves staff with a plan for action, sometimes called a *strategic plan* or a *school improvement plan*.

For this plan to become a reality, staff members must often increase their own competencies in areas associated with the desired outcomes, such as their technology skills or knowledge of how to differentiate instruction. Because staff are working with a site-based school improvement plan, the plan for professional growth should also be site based. This approach allows staff to configure a professional development agenda that supports them in attaining their school outcomes and in addressing their individual needs. The first step in developing a site-based staff development plan is to identify the competencies and needs of individual staff members. Staff members examine their own strengths and weaknesses and reflect on where they need to grow to help make the school vision a reality. By looking first at individual needs, each staff member is challenged to identify areas for growth that are both personally meaningful and beneficial to the students.

Questions to Identify Areas for Professional Growth

• How do I need to grow to contribute to the realization of our school's vision?

• What do I need to learn?

Next, staff members openly share their interests with their colleagues by searching for common interests. Processes that help staff discover shared professional interests vary from formal to informal activities. Collaborative learning teams might develop naturally out of lunchroom discussions, or they might emerge from a multistep process of identifying, reflecting, and group decision making. Any process used at this stage should encourage staff members to voice their interests, as well as promote active listening among staff members. Tools 3 and 4, "Affinity" and "Open Space," in Part III, "Tools for Learning," support individual expression of interests, as well as common themes. Once all interests are in the public arena, each staff member selects a specific topic of study that is personally meaningful and announces it to the group. As the process progresses, staff members who have similar professional

development interests form clusters, which eventually become collaborative learning teams. When the topics for collaborative learning are funneled from individual interests to collective interests, the final decision represents the shared curiosity of all team members.

Self-organizing into collaborative learning teams can be a rather messy process. The following criteria offer some guidance for forming collaborative learning teams:

• Collaborative learning teams are self-organized around topics of study that are meaningful to the individual and the vision of the school.

• Membership is open to all members of the school community, including paraprofessionals, specialists, parents, and administrators.

• Membership is voluntary.

• Membership is flexible, allowing members to switch groups, leave groups, or join groups at any point in time.

• A final date for forming teams should be identified, at which time a list of topics and team members is posted.

The case study of Hayward Elementary School shows how a school staff formed collaborative learning teams (see box, "Hayward Elementary School").

Introduction to the Collaborative Learning Process

Teachers learn just as their students do: by studying, doing, and reflecting; by collaborating with other teachers; by looking closely at students and their work; and by sharing what they see. . . . Good settings for teacher

Hayward Elementary School: A Case Study

Hayward Elementary School represents a fictitious school, yet it is based on the experiences of the authors as they worked with collaborative learning teams in elementary schools.

The tone of the conversations among the teaching staff at Hayward Elementary School has been the same for several months now: concerned, frustrated, and anxious. The student population of 385 at Hayward has been gradually changing over the past several years to include the following:

- More families whose home language is Spanish.
- An addition of a primary-age class for students with mild mental retardation (MR).
- Thirty-two students diagnosed as learning disabled in grades 1 through 5 (an increase of about 25 percent over the past two years).
- A significant increase in the number of students who have an attention-deficit disorder (ADD) diagnosis in grades 2 through 5.

The school staff has also changed and grown to include personnel who have expertise in teaching students with MR, limited English proficiency, and learning disabilities. Spurred on by the passing of the 1997 reauthorization of the Individuals with Disabilities Education Act, the state's Department of Education is emphasizing the integration of all students into general education programs, yet no statewide model for integrated schooling has been proposed. Each school can design its own model of service delivery, based on the needs of its students.

A few months ago, Hayward staff, parents, and community members developed a shared vision. They decided that they wanted to be known as an inclusive school where (1) all children are special and (2) all children learn together to the maximum extent possible. The school is organized by grade levels, with separate classes or pullout programs for children with learning disabilities and other special needs. Moving from this segregated service delivery model to an inclusive school where students with special needs receive support and services in the general education classroom will require significant growth and change on the part of the staff. Establishing a staff development plan that addresses areas of need is one of the school's top priorities.

The principal used the "Affinity" tool (Tool 3 in Part III) to develop the school's professional development plan. First, each staff member reflected on the following question: "If our school is to become a quality inclusive school, how do I need to grow and change?" On Post-it Notes, each staff member wrote several ideas for professional growth. Group members then presented their ideas in a round-robin fashion, sticking their Post-its on a big, empty wall and clustering the ideas that were similar. Through this personal and collective reflection process, five broad topics for professional study emerged:

- Transitions.
- Peer interactions.
- Parent partnerships.
- Teaching students with ADD.
- Coteaching.

As a final step, each staff member selected one of the five topics that was personally meaningful. Staff members with shared interests formed collaborative learning teams that would spend the next nine months studying and experimenting together.

learning provide lots of opportunities for research and inquiry, for trying and testing, for talking about and evaluating the results of learning and teaching (Darling-Hammond, 1997, pp. 319–320).

In the collaborative learning process, a group of people address the question "What are we going to learn together?" Collaborative learning teams may answer that question in many ways. For example, they may expand their knowledge in a specific area, such as the impact of brain research on education; they may test new classroom strategies, such as reading theater; or they may design a new model for instructional delivery, such as multi-age classrooms. The topics of study are derived from the felt needs of the team members and relate to the vision of the school.

The collaborative learning process has five stages: (1) define, (2) explore, (3) experiment, (4) reflect, and (5) share (see Figure 5.1). Time spent at each stage of the cycle is proportional to its size in Figure 5.1. For example, the "define" stage takes about one-eighth of the total time, whereas the "explore" stage is about three-eighths of the total.

A significant commitment of time is needed to complete one cycle of the collaborative learning process. Learning teams at Hayward Elementary School spent approximately 10 months completing the cycle. Team meetings varied from once a month to once a week, each lasting about two hours. Staff also spent time visiting exemplary programs, going to conferences, consulting with experts, and researching new practices. Figure 5.2 offers a sample time frame for a 9-month collaborative

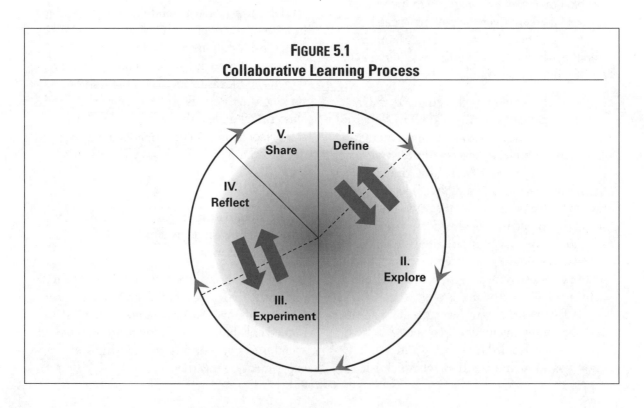

FIGURE 5.1
Collaborative Learning Process

	Figure 5.2	
	Time Line of the Collaborative Learning Process	
Stage of Collaborative Learning Process	**Sample Time Line**	**Participating Group**
Establish a Staff Development Plan	Month 1	Schoolwide
Form Collaborative Learning Teams	Month 2	Schoolwide
Define	Month 2	Collaborative Learning Team
Explore	Months 3–5	Collaborative Learning Team
Experiment	Months 6–9	Collaborative Learning Team
Reflect	Months 7–9	Collaborative Learning Team
Share	Month 10	Schoolwide

learning cycle. The more times the staff repeats this cyclical process, the more likely it is that "teachers as learners" will become a part of the school culture.

Having facilitators guide team members through the collaborative learning process and support them in their research and experimentation is advantageous. The facilitator can be someone outside the team, a member of the team, or team members who rotate the position. Facilitators benefit from having support and guidance from the school leadership, as well as from meeting regularly with other facilitators to reflect on their group's progress and review the next steps of the collaborative learning process.

Stages of the Collaborative Learning Process

Stage 1: Define

Create shared meaning about the topic and specific terms. At the onset of the collaborative learning process, each group member chooses to be a part of the group because of a personal interest in the topic of study. In the beginning, the topic probably has different meanings for different group members. For example, transitions, peer interaction, and teaching students with attention-deficit disorder (ADD) are all common ideas in education, yet they probably mean significantly different things to different people. Several strategies are helpful in developing a shared meaning among team members (see box, "Strategies for Promoting Shared Meaning").

You can also encourage shared meaning by having group members write the definitions of words that are confusing and then share their ideas. The understanding that emerges from discussing personal interpretations of words and topics helps create common ground for the group's collaborative work.

Further define topic of study. Once an acceptable level of shared meaning exists among team members, they can more precisely define the topic of study. For example, one group may refine an interest in "transition" to reflect an interest in "transitioning children with disabilities from grade to grade." To another group, "peer interaction" may now mean "peer interaction during free-choice time." The topics of study become more focused as group members develop a common understanding of their topic and articulate their personal priorities for professional growth.

Strategies for Promoting Shared Meaning

• Slow down the conversation by asking a question before giving an opinion.
• Draw reasoning from a peer: "Can you help me understand your thinking?"
• Make sure you understand another's point of view: "Am I correct in saying you think _____?"
• Encourage others to explore your idea: "What do you think about what I just said?"

Formulate a question that addresses the topic of study. Having the topic of study formatted in a question rather than a statement is based on the teacher-research model (Calhoun, 1993). The question is purposefully broad in scope so as to encourage a slowing down of solution-seeking behavior and a furthering of research and exploration behavior. This initial broad question can be easily configured by asking, "What can we do differently to . . . [fill in topic of study]?" When you begin with a more global question, you invite all team members to express their multiple interests. At this point, the challenge is to keep all members of a

learning team talking about what personally excites them. Teams must realize that their global question is only a starter question to help kick off the discussion-and-exploration process. Later, they will work together to mold a more precise question that continues to embrace multiple interests (see box, "Questions to Help Formulate a Topic of Study").

At Hayward Elementary School, one team of kindergarten, 1st, and 2nd grade teachers wanted to learn more about teaching children with ADD. To create some shared understanding of their topic, team members discussed the meaning of ADD and the characteristics of children with ADD. Finally, they configured a broad question from which to launch their exploring phase: "What can we do differently to accommodate the needs of students with ADD?"

Questions to Help Formulate a Topic of Study

• What can we do differently in the area we are studying?
• How can we increase our capacity in this area?

Also, a collaborative learning team made up of preschool regular and special education teachers and assistant teachers began their inquiry into the topic of peer interaction by doing a "Shared Meaning Chart" (see Figure 5.3). This chart helped them clarify terms such as "peer interaction" and "strategies." They then formulated their ideas into a question: "What can we do differently to encourage successful peer interactions?"

FIGURE 5.3
Shared Meaning Chart
Hayward Elementary School

Write your thoughts and examples of what these words or ideas mean to you.

Peer Interaction	Strategies
• children playing with one another • children sharing a toy • children communicating, verbally and nonverbally	• activities • environmental arrangements • teacher interventions • props or materials

Share topic of study and question with school community. To conclude this stage, each team drafts a statement of its topic of study, its question, and the relationship between the area of interest and the school vision. This *charter*, which is not a final plan but rather the first written rendering of the topic of study, helps the team translate its ideas into writing (see Figure 5.4 on p. 50). Each team presents its charter to the entire school for feedback. Connecting the learning team's intentions with the thinking of the entire staff helps maintain an alignment of purpose and goals throughout the school community. Teams also seek administrative approval at this time to ensure that each topic of study has the support of the school leader.

Stage 2: Explore

Develop a game plan. The "explore" stage accounts for a significant amount of time— about 40 percent—in the collaborative learning process. During this stage, team members engage in three major tasks:

1. Identify current practices.
2. Explore new practices.
3. Refine the question.

Teamwork is expedited when the team begins this phase by designing an overarching plan and time line for exploring. An adaptation of the "Game Plan" visual tool (The Grove Consultants International, 1995)* can help the group specify methods and a sequence for exploring, as well as visualize how the plan relates to the schoolwide goal. The "peer interaction" team at Hayward Elementary began to explore by creating a game plan. The plan listed ways the team wanted to explore the topic, including reading journal articles, reflecting on strategies currently being used, and visiting other classrooms (see Figure 5.5 on p. 51). Individuals worked in pairs to look in different areas for information.

Identify current practices and underlying assumptions. In this phase, teams investigate what they are doing and why. "What" and "why" go hand in hand as team members identify current practice and then discuss the thinking behind the practice. At Hayward Elementary School, students with ADD spend 15 minutes every 2 hours in a pullout, small-group situation. As team members explored the question "Why do we do this?" they discovered their assumption was that regular changes in the setting enhance the ability of ADD

*Adapted by permission from The Grove Consultants International, P.O. Box 29391, 1000 Torney Ave., San Francisco, CA 94129-0391; phones: 1-800-494-7683; 1-415-561-2500; World Wide Web: http://www.grove.com

students to learn. Through careful examination of current practices and underlying assumptions, the group had the baseline information necessary to move forward (see box, "Questions About Current Practice").

FIGURE 5.4
Charter

Topic for Learning: *Peer Interaction*
Members: *Ramona, Terry, Lyn, Maureen, Jill, Amy, and Vibha*

1. What is our topic of study? *To increase the number of strategies for parents and teachers to promote peer interactions among children with and without special needs.*
2. How does this idea contribute to our school's vision? *It promotes social integration.*
3. What is our question? *What can we do differently to encourage successful peer interactions?*
4. What resources will we need to complete our project (time, materials, training, consultation, other)? *Articles and books, site visits, expert's visit to our school.*

Approval: *Marianne McDermott*   Date: *9/30/98*
Principal

Explore new ideas and underlying assumptions. At the exploring stage, people spend a great deal of time and energy searching for new information, sharing information, and reflecting on what the information means to the team. Teams often begin by identifying familiar resources to explore—familiar in that people know about these resources but have not yet had time to investigate them (see box, "Ways to Look for New Ideas").

When teams are investigating, they discover and share new ideas. Members consider

Ways to Look for New Ideas

- Observe exemplary models
- Interview experts
- Research and read
- Attend conferences
- Explore the Internet
- Network with peers

the new ideas and talk about the underlying assumptions. Over time, they realize that there are many different ways of thinking about problems. For example, the team investigating how to teach students with ADD realized that changing settings does not necessarily help students with ADD. For some students, it is more advantageous to consider frequent changes in activity within the same setting. This realization opens a different line of thinking and fuels the generative learning process among team members (see box, "Questions for Exploring New Ideas," p. 53).

The "Exploration Grid" (see Figure 5.6, p. 52) and the "KWL Chart" (see Figure 5.7, p. 54) are good tools to use during the exploring stage. (KWL means "What We Know, What We Want to Learn, and What We Learned.") Both tools encourage the group to

Questions About Current Practice

- What am I doing? or What are we doing?
- What theories and assumptions drive my/our actions?

		FIGURE 5.5 Game Plan		
Define	**Explore**	**Experiment**	**Reflect**	**Share**
* Peer interaction * Indicator of success * Area of play to focus on	* Other programs * Journals and books * Local and state conferences * Video * Internet	* Changing environments * Teacher strategies * Home strategies	* Use video to document and reflect * Use a child study approach	* Share with parents and community preschools * Keep informal * Bring illustration to share
Current Status: Children without disabilities play together and ignore children with disabilities the majority of the time.			**Vision:** Children with and without disabilities spontaneously play together during center time	
October	**Nov.–Jan.**	**Feb.–Mar.**	**April–May**	**June**

think about several aspects of study simultaneously and facilitate a shifting of focus among current practice, new ideas, and next steps.

Refine question. Before a team moves into the "experiment" stage, participants again narrow and fine-tune the question. The refining process helps the team create a "do able" project that has a finite focus and definable parameters. This process requires team members to funnel ideas to the core interest of the group (see box, "Questions That Help Share Insights and Refine the Team's Question," p. 56).

In the case of the "peer interaction" group, the question changed from "What can we do differently to encourage peer interactions during free-choice time?" to "How does the environment affect peer interaction during free-choice time?" The "teaching-children-with-ADD" team changed its question from "What can we do differently to accommodate the needs of students with ADD?" to "How can we adapt the classroom to keep the students with ADD continuously engaged in learning?" In the next stage, "experiment," team members design and test one or more interventions that address the refined question.

Stage 3: Experiment

Design action based on the question and a set of assumptions. The experimenting stage is the time to try something new. During this stage, teams need to remember that learning is an active process for adults, as well as for children. The learner is continually constructing

FIGURE 5.6
Exploration Grid
Hayward Elementary School

Team Question: *What can we do differently to accommodate the needs of children with attention-deficit disorder (ADD)?*

What challenges are we currently experiencing and why?	What is currently working for us and why?	What new ideas are we playing with and why?	What will we continue to investigate and why?	What is next?
• For students with ADD, the instruction becomes choppy because they frequently move in and out of the classroom. Questions exist about who is ultimately responsible for the progress of students with ADD.	• Team planning session with general and special educator helps get us on the same page.	• Having students with ADD switch activities within the room rather than move rooms might provide less fragmentation.	• Literature and consultants' opinions about best strategies for working with students with ADD offer new ideas.	• Visit schools where students with ADD are in the regular classroom. * Do a literature search.

new ideas and theories. Team members construct knowledge through trial and error—through thinking and doing. Learning takes time, and accepting mistakes is part of the learning experience.

In the experimenting stage, the team decides what actions to take based on their question and the assumptions from which they are operating (see box, "Questions for Designing an Experiment," p. 56). Articulating the underlying assumptions is challenging but contributes significantly to the learning because the team must explain the thinking behind its actions. For example, the "peer interaction" group modified its environment by integrating tables into the centers; this modification was based on the following assumptions: (1) young children interact more frequently when in smaller groups, and (2) tables tend to draw small groups of children together.

The team may design a singular experiment, or it can take a variety of actions. For example, actions consistent with the question "How does the environment affect peer interactions during free-choice time?" might be the following:

• Integrate tables into centers.
• Put two sets of contact paper "feet" (child-sized foot shapes) on the floor at each side of the water table, to help children space themselves while playing together.

• Have one or two sociodramatic props, such as a farm or car wash in the block area.

• Arrange two easels side by side in the art area.

The team may decide to try one change in each room or have several classrooms make the same change. The team must carefully consider the potential consequences of all experiments before the trial period. Team members should consult with the school leader throughout the design phase.

We encourage teams to have a mechanism to help them coordinate the actions of their team members. The "Action Plan Grid " (see Figure 5.8, p. 55) is one way to document action, individual responsibilities, and results.

Observe and document results. Observing and documenting results help feed the group reflection process. We encourage members of the group to gather ongoing data that answer a simple question: "What is happening?" Methods of documentation might include photos, video, anecdotal records, work samples, interviews, and surveys.

Whenever possible, teams should encourage parents and professionals representing

---

Questions for Exploring New Ideas

• What new ideas have we heard about?

• Where will we search for information about these new ideas?

• What did we find in our searching?

• What theories and assumptions are behind these ideas?

---

different roles and disciplines to offer their perspectives on the experiment. Having a variety of individuals observe and document the results of the experiment adds richness and depth to the data.

During the "experiment" stage, the "peer interaction" group at Hayward Elementary changed the environment in the art area in one classroom. Team members labeled the art supplies and set them out on accessible shelves; placed two double easels side by side; and put a large table with four chairs in the middle of the art area. Team members documented peer interactions using anecdotal notes and photographs. After a few weeks, the team made similar changes in all its classrooms and documented the results by videotaping peer interactions. After reviewing and discussing the video, the team refined its interventions.

Stage 4: Reflect

Reflection is the gift we give ourselves, not passive thought that lolls aimlessly in our minds, but an effort we must approach with rigor, with some purpose in mind, and in some formal way, so as to reveal the wisdom embedded in our experience (Killion & Todnem, 1991, p. 14).

Real learning occurs in analyzing actions or experiments. This analysis deepens understanding of work and informs discussions and decisions about future practice. The function of individual reflection is to inquire more deeply into one's self and one's actions. The function of team reflection is to consider multiple perspectives and glean insights that will drive future action. Openness to the thoughts of others and the freedom to express oneself are

FIGURE 5.7
KWL Chart
Hayward Elementary School

Team Question: *What can we do differently to encourage successful peer interactions?*

What We *Know*	What We *Want* to Know	What We *Learned*
• Children without disabilities tend to play together more often during free-play time, leaving out the children with disabilities. • Most of our children with disabilities have a difficult time sharing their toys, entering a play situation, and carrying on an ongoing communication exchange. • Parents of children with disabilities in our classes are very anxious about the behavior of their children and their acceptance by the other children.	• Strategies to help the children with disabilities be more a part of the play situation, even though they may not have good communication skills. • Ways to inform parents on a regular basis about the children that their child is playing with. • Ways to encourage parents to promote informal play situations between children in the class outside of school. • Environmental factors that would promote successful peer interactions, especially for those children who are withdrawn or aggressive.	• The digitized camera can help keep parents informed of interactions in the classroom. We can include pictures of the day's events in our report that we send home at the end of school. • Sensorimotor activities are prime for children of different ability and communication levels to play together. • Scripting is a good strategy to help children learn common play sequences in the housekeeping areas or at the sand and water table.

crucial to the team reflection process. Failed experiments should not result in blame; rather, failure provides an opportunity to delve deeper as a team into the question being considered.

Individual Reflection. Because individual reflection provides the food for group reflection, it is an ideal place to begin the reflective process. By looking at the data, people can compare the actual results of the experiment with the anticipated results: "I thought that would happen, but in actuality, this happened. What does that tell me?" (see box, "Individual Reflection Questions").

Keeping a personal journal of observations and insights is a powerful mechanism for individual reflection. Here are several formats to guide personal reflection:

• **3–2–1 Reflection.** This activity offers a short and sweet format for participants to document their thoughts. The categories or types of ideas vary, depending on the purpose of reflection:

3 things I learned.
2 ideas I want to pursue.
1 question I have.

• **What, What, What.** Participants respond to a variety of "what" questions. The questions vary, depending on the purpose of reflection

– What did I learn that was helpful?
– What challenges did I encounter?
– What got me through them?
– What did I learn in the process?

• **Observations and Interpretations.** This format is particularly useful when observing a child or peer. The observer documents observations and examines personal interpretations of the situation (see form, top of p. 56).

Group Reflection. Group reflection unfolds in many different ways. The lesson that one team member learns often stirs new thinking in other team members. The collective capacity of the group to listen, think, and invent new practices is often surprising. The "peer interaction" team at Hayward Elementary shared results by watching the video together and then comparing what actually happened with what team members thought would happen. Then one person reported results on a specific child and asked others to help her interpret the results. Some members needed more time to collect results, but all seemed inspired to keep going after reaping the benefits of the group reflection time.

		FIGURE 5.8 Action Plan Grid Hayfield Elementary School "Peer Interaction" Team		
What do we want to do?	**What actions do we need to take?**	**Who is responsible for each action?**	**By when?**	**Observation**
Change one part of the environment in each room.	Room 14: Integrate tables into art, literacy, housekeeping, and discovery centers	Lynn	12/1	Table in art area needs to be much bigger. More sharing at tables than on floor.
	Room 15: Put contact paper feet on the floor at each side of the water table.	Marta	12/1	Works great for crowd control.
	Room 16: Coordinate the sociodramatic props in the block area with the current theme.	Vibha	12/1	Cleanup is much easier. Also easier to facilitate theme-related language.
	Room 17: Arrange two art easels side by side in the art area.	Christine	12/1	Not much use in the first week.

What I observed was . . .	My thoughts and interpretations were . . .

Diversity of perspective also enriches the reflective process because each person contributes a unique way of viewing the learning process. For example, a team composed of a regular classroom teacher, a learning disabilities specialist, a parent, and an occupational therapist will probably generate a broader range of questions, reflections, and strategies about a specific dilemma than a more homogeneous team, such as a grade-level team (see box, "Group Reflection Questions" for some starting points). Part III, "Tools for Learning," includes "Think, Pair, Share" (Tool 5), an activity for group reflection that encourages team members to "stop and think" together.

Questions That Help Share Insights and Refine the Team's Question

- What did we learn?
- What are we interested in continuing to explore?
- What question will best guide our work?

Questions for Designing an Experiment

- What do we want to do?
- Why do we think this is a good idea?
- How are we going to accomplish this?

Stage 5: Share

True professionals engage in disciplined inquiry: they test their theories, share their results, and, consequently, learn from one another (Sagor, 1995, p. 25).

The sharing stage offers an opportunity for learning teams to communicate their insights, share the knowledge they have acquired, and discuss the process of learning together. Sharing insights helps build the capacity of all staff in the school to better serve children and their families. As learning teams gain expertise in their topic of study, they become in-house consultants and resources to their school community. As staff members share their new knowledge and skills, they develop an increased sense of pride about who they are as a community.

Team members can share their insights and knowledge in many ways, including a slide

Question for Documenting Results

- What is happening?

show, video, workshop discussion group, newsletter, or a group presentation. Some groups may prefer to use a "poster session" format in which groups display their information and the staff roam from table to table to gather information and ask questions. Regardless of the process, sharing their insights challenges teams to synthesize their work and organize it into a format that colleagues can understand. Synthesizing and articulating their knowledge and insights helps bring team members' learning to a higher level of understanding (see box, "Questions to Help Discuss Collaborative Work," p. 58, for some ways to begin this synthesis). As team members go through the process, many teams come to realize they are no longer replicating someone else's ideas, but rather they have constructed a strategy that is unique to their situation and that meets the needs of their children. The sense of being able to *invent* best practice rather than just *replicate* the ideas of others is empowering.

Individual Reflection Questions

- Did I fulfill my intent?
- What did I learn?
- How has my perspective changed as a result of this experience?

At Hayward Elementary, the "peer interaction" group decided to have an informal discussion after school to share insights. The group invited the members of the early childhood program in their school, including preschool through 1st grade staff and specialists, as well as teachers from community preschool programs. Team members shared the peer-interaction strategies and discussed the results. The attendees actively participated by relating their experiences using peer-interaction strategies and seeking more information about the strategies being presented.

Group Reflection Questions

- What did we accomplish?
- What would we do differently?
- How does this inform our next step?
- What was important to us as learners?

The sharing stage also offers an opportunity for teams to share lessons learned about collaborative learning. John Browne, Chief Economic Officer of British Petroleum, advises that every time an action or experience is repeated, it should be critiqued to see how it can be done more efficiently and effectively the next time (Prokesch, 1997). If collaborative learning is to become part of professional development, staff must take time to examine and refine their ability to learn collaboratively (see box, "Questions for Reflecting on the Collaborative Learning Process," p. 58).

☞   ☞   ☞

In *A Simpler Way*, Wheatley and Kellner-Rogers (1996) share this story:

> The tower-building termites of Africa and Australia accomplish little

when they act alone; they dig only lowly piles of dirt. But as they attract other termites to their vicinity, a collective forms. As a group, they become builders of immense towers—engineering marvels filled with arches, tunnels, air conditioning systems, and specialized chambers. These intricate towers are the largest structures on earth if you consider the size of their builders. But if we observed only the individual termites, we could never predict what they do as a collective. It wouldn't matter how long we observed them as individuals (p. 68).

The authors assert that, like the termites, we can't predict what we might accomplish as a collective. We discover what we are capable of as we go along.

Joining a collaborative learning team is like taking a leap of faith. Team members have some guarantee that the group is going to learn about something that its members are "more or less" interested in. But how the experiment is going to turn out or how the group is going to function as a learning team remains unknown. On the other side of these doubts is the possibility that something wonderful will happen—maybe the team will find a better way to help

kids and families by using a new instructional practice or will help children with ADD become more successful in school.

Wonderful things can happen for children and families as a result of the collaborative learning process. Yet creating miraculous results for children and families is not the whole story. Other miracles occur as a result of the collaborative learning process: Staff get to know each other in new and different ways, parents become respected members of professional learning teams, hierarchical boundaries between teaching roles are dissolved, and an increased empathy for difficulties across grade levels and throughout the school emerges.

What each collaborative learning team accomplishes as a collective cannot be predicted by observing the individuals on the team. In the collaborative learning process, the whole *is* greater than the sum of the parts. By working together, something greater can be created. The collaborative learning process is a method for releasing the synergy that resides in all our schools. Let's not waste it.

Questions to Help Discuss Collaborative Work

- What has our team accomplished, created, or learned?
- How did we accomplish this?
- What effect does our work have on teachers, children, and families?
- What next steps might we take?

Questions for Reflecting on the Collaborative Learning Process

- What did we learn about "learning collaboratively"?
- How has collaborative learning enhanced the capacity of our team to provide quality instruction to our children?

Enhancing Capacity to Learn

Learning collaboratively is a complex process that requires learners to understand themselves, their motives, and their thoughts and beliefs, as well as the motives, thoughts, and beliefs of others. It also requires merging of individual interests into a collective aspiration. Finally, it requires a group "work ethic" or way of behaving that creates a bond of trust, belonging, and purposefulness among group members.

People involved in collaborative learning can address these complexities more easily when they take time to build relationships and plan a method for learning together. Learners may decide to establish ground rules or specific communication guidelines. They may adopt processes that support generative thinking and reflection. This chapter focuses on tools and techniques that support groups in creating powerful ways of relating to one another.

Developing Interdependence

Collaborative learning necessitates interaction among groups of individuals. The potential of the interactions varies significantly, depending on the degree of *interdependence* among group members. Steven Covey (1989) defines interdependence as "the paradigm of *we*—we can do it, we can cooperate, we can combine our talents and abilities and create something greater together" (p. 49). He goes on to say, "Interdependence opens up worlds of possibilities for deep, rich, meaningful associations, for geometrically increased productivity, for serving, for contributing, for learning, for growing" (p. 187).

Developing interdependence within a group is a time-consuming process that is enhanced when each team member possesses a solid understanding of one's self (see box, "Questions for Self-Understanding").

This self-knowledge is then combined with looking outward—noticing the gifts and talents of others, as well as valuing the diversity of thought and experience expressed by the group. Understanding ourselves and understanding others support collaborative learning teams in developing interdependence.

Questions for Self-Understanding

- Who am I?
- What do I believe?
- What am I willing to contribute?

Understanding Self

Deeply held beliefs, values, and assumptions exert a powerful influence on our thoughts and actions (Caine & Caine, 1997) and form our personal worldview. Our worldview is rooted in life experiences that stretch back to our early years. These experiences create a lens through which we process new thoughts and experiences.

Our worldview or way of seeing influences our interpretation of the daily events in our lives. From the many stimuli that are constantly bombarding our senses, we pay attention to the stimuli we consider important. We select these stimuli because they are of interest to us. They may be compatible with our underlying assumptions and, therefore, affirming; or they may be incompatible, therefore creating a sense of disequilibrium. The following reflection by a teacher demonstrates the way the same stimuli can affirm two different sets of assumptions or worldviews:

> Two teachers are watching the same children play. The first teacher sees the children exploring their world as they collect sticks, dig with them, test their trajectory, and hear the sounds they make. The other teacher sees the children out of control as they collect sticks, spear them into the ground, throw them blindly, and bang them on the playground equipment. The worldview of the first teacher is shaped by her belief that children learn through active exploration. The worldview of the second is based on the belief that young children with sticks are dangerous. Each teacher has processed the stimuli in a way that is congruent with her personal worldview and is likely to take action based on the meaning she has attributed to the situation—the first teacher might expand the child's thinking while the second might briskly outlaw the use of sticks.

Personal worldviews exist below the level of awareness, where they often remain unexamined and untested. Examining and talking about our personal worldviews is a difficult task, particularly as we mature and our perceptions become buried in years of collected experiences. An understanding of how our past shapes our current actions and decisions is key to understanding ourselves. By identifying the frame through which we routinely view an experience, we become more aware of the assumptions that shape our views, as another teacher observed:

> I may perceive a colleague as difficult to deal with on the basis of past experiences. Because of that perception, I view many of her comments such as, "I don't understand your idea," as negative, unsupportive, and challenging. Once I realize that I listen to her through a negative lens, I have a new freedom to choose how I interpret what she says—I am better able to really listen to what she is saying rather than reactivate my past feeling and experiences.

Similarly, our professional thinking is shaped by the pedagogical beliefs and assumptions that we have internalized. Take the concept "learning." Here are two views of learning—behaviorist and constructivist—that are opposite in many ways:

- If your thinking about learning is heavily influenced by behavorist theory, you view learning as a stimulus-response process that is externally reinforced with a system of rewards and punishments. To behaviorists, terms like *operant conditioning, reinforcement schedules,* and *antecedent events* are central to the learning process.

• If you are a constructivist, learning is an internal process in which individuals construct their own views of reality by acting on and interacting with the world. To constructivists, terms like *play, active learning,* and *mediation* are central to learning.

Imagine how difficult it might be for teachers to collaborate if one teacher views learning through a behaviorist perspective, and the other through a constructivist perspective. One teacher believes that learning occurs best in a teacher-directed classroom where children accumulate knowledge and facts that are dispensed by the teacher; the other teacher believes that learning occurs best in a learner-centered, active classroom where the teacher poses problems, encourages interaction, and serves as a resource to facilitate learning.

Understanding ourselves requires us to identify and "own" the assumptions and beliefs that shape our worldview, whether it is our professional worldview or our personal worldview. In the process of making our worldview more visible to ourselves and others, we increase our capability to discuss and modify our assumptions, as well as let go of those assumptions that no longer serve us well.

Personal reflection heightens our awareness of the beliefs and assumptions that shape our worldview and guide our actions. In *The Fifth Discipline Fieldbook,* Charlotte Roberts (Senge, Kleiner, Roberts, Ross, & Smith, 1994, p. 396) suggests a few questions that might lead to

reflective thinking about our motives for action (see box, "Questions for Examining Our Beliefs and Assumptions").

Questions for Examining Our Beliefs and Assumptions

• What strong opinions do you hold about this topic? Where did these opinions come from?
• What observable data can you bring to this discussion?
• Are you willing to be influenced?
• What is your vision for a satisfactory outcome for this issue?

When we ask and answer questions like these, we may break up some of the biases and unquestioned assumptions that we bring to group discussions.

Understanding Others

To know one's self is wisdom, but to know one's neighbor is genius.
—MINNA ANTRIM (1861–1950),
AMERICAN EPIGRAMMIST

No two individuals are exactly alike. When people have similar histories, experiences, or education, we often anticipate compatibility. When differences are apparent, we often expect struggle and contention. Yet we know the presence of different points of view within a group can actually lead to creative solutions.

A collaborative learning environment encourages people to voice different perspectives, yet an element of risk is present when we unveil our thinking to a group of colleagues. An essential ingredient in collaborative learning environments is an atmosphere of trust. *Trust* in this context refers to the safety level in the group. In a trusting environment, the group is willing to consider the diverse opinions of others. They respect, value, and appreciate the ideas and beliefs of their colleagues. Members are able to speak openly— to express their opinions and beliefs without loss of status or the fear of reprisal.

In a trusting environment, people are safe to say what's on their mind, seek the counsel of others, and experiment with new ideas. This environment offers a place where judgment about spoken communication and actions are suspended. Such an atmosphere invites participation. The following elements are present in environments characterized by high levels of trust:

- *Openness*—inviting all group members to participate by offering information, ideas, thoughts, feelings, and reactions.
- *Sharing*—offering materials and resources to help the group move toward its goal.
- *Acceptance*—communicating positive regard to other group members about their contributions to the work.
- *Support*—recognizing the strengths and capabilities of group members.
- *Cooperative intention*—expecting all members to function cooperatively and collaboratively to achieve the group purpose.

Developing a trusting atmosphere occurs little by little. The following activities encourage the building of trust by asking people to share information about themselves:

My Treasure Box. This team activity brings events that have shaped our lives to the forefront. Team members fill boxes or bags with objects and pictures that have significance to them and then share with the group their special items and the reasons they chose them. The explanation of choices begins to disclose the values and beliefs of the team members.

Similarities and Differences. Two people, paired together, are asked to name something about each other that is the same and something that is different. For example, the choice could be a physical attribute, a philosophy, a historical fact. This begins the connecting process by acknowledging sameness and difference and foreshadows how difficult it can be for group members to talk about themselves and about differences.

Self-disclosure (Sapon-Shevin, 1992, p. 30). The questions in this activity encourage risk taking and personal exposure by asking people to respond to more value-laden questions—questions that discuss individual strengths and weaknesses. In answering these questions, participants may find complementary skills and interests:

- What are three things I am really good at?
- What are three things I have trouble with?
- What are some ways I can help people?
- What are some things I need help with, and what kind of help would I like?

Embracing individual differences is another component of understanding others. Seeing differences as a *contribution*, not a *detriment*, brings a sense of value to the uniqueness of each person in the group. The presence of positive regard encourages members to share their passions and idiosyncrasies, and stimulates the creativity that arises from full engagement and self-expression. Learning increases—and seems to explode—when team members are free to contribute to and learn from the diverse perspectives in their group.

Creating a Team Sculpture. This activity emphasizes the contributions each person brings to the team and ties them together into a whole. Teams create a sculpture that represents their team's identity—its diversity, commonalities, and accomplishments. Here are examples of materials that teams can use in this activity: a sheet of foamcore or cardboard for each team, Styrofoam pieces, pipecleaners, clothespins, yarn, string, ribbon, markers, colored and textured papers, stickers, glue, toothpicks, and tape. Steps in the process are as follows:

- Each member shares a personal trait.
- Members discuss traits, looking for similarities and differences.
- Members translate their ideas into a sculpture that represents their team's identity.
- Members title their sculpture.
- Each team shares the sculpture with other teams.

Let's String Along (Scannell & Newstrom, 1991, p. 287). This activity brings to light the interdependent nature of our work and elucidates the importance of having a versatile, diverse group of coworkers. Each group has a ball of string or yarn, and group members stand in a circle. One group member holds the ball of string and ties the end to her wrist. She throws the ball of string to someone whom she is dependent on and states the nature of that dependency. The process continues as different people hold the string and throw the ball to other members of the group.

Developing a sense of interdependence requires that we come to know ourselves, our biases, and our assumptions; that we trust each other enough to share personal viewpoints, experience, and information; and that we come to embrace and celebrate our differences.

Communication Norms That Support Collaborative Learning

Clearly stated communication norms contribute to an atmosphere of trust when people are learning collaboratively. Communication norms are *shared expectations* about how group members will communicate with each other. They provide guidelines that support collaborative exploration, discovery, and reflection.

In many groups, members talk "at" one another. Communication consists of each member presenting his point of view and defending it with more thoughts when challenged. In this talking "at" model, the speaker's work is the skillful display of his ideas; the group's work is to choose the best of the ideas presented. Conversely, collaborative learning relies on the ability of team members to talk "with" each other, working together to understand and mold the group's many ideas into a new whole.

Belenky and colleagues (1986) have named these two types of talk *didactic talking* and *really talking*. Didactic talking offers little or no attempt among group members to combine their thoughts and ideas to acquire new levels of understanding. The practice of really talking asks group members to share ideas in a way that ideas can grow. Really talking happens when members share from deep within their own experience and embrace the ideas and experiences of others. *Collaborative learning flourishes in an environment filled with really talking.* This section discusses five communication norms that facilitate really talking:

- Listen carefully.
- Share relevant information.
- Develop shared meaning.
- Make assumptions explicit.
- Decide by consensus.

We offer a word of warning before we discuss the specific communication norms: *Communication norms cannot be imposed on a group.* The group, as a group, draws forth norms that are meaningful for it. The norms are based on the values, expectations, and past experiences of the group members. Communication norms must be clear to all members. Once the group identifies norms, group members should practice the norms to ensure that everybody in the group can recognize and use them in conversation. Groups increase their ability to use the norms masterfully when they incorporate a time and method for group reflection and feedback into their team meetings. "Communication Norms for Collaborative Groups," Tool 6 in Part III, "Tools for Learning," can help groups explore effective communication norms.

Listen Carefully

Listen
I do not know if you have ever
　　examined how you listen,
it doesn't matter to what, whether to a
　　bird, to the wind in the leaves,
to the rushing waters, or how you listen
　　in a dialogue with yourself,
to your conversation in various
　　relationships with your
　　　intimate friends,
your wife or husband. . . .
If we try to listen, we find it
　　extraordinarily difficult
because we are always projecting our
　　opinions and ideas,
our prejudices, our background, our
　　　inclinations, our impulses;
when they dominate we hardly listen
　　at all to what is being said. . .
In that state there is no value at all.
　One listens and therefore learns,
　　only in a state of attention,
　　a state of silence,
　　in which this whole background
　　is in abeyance, is quiet;
　　then, it seems to me, it is
　　possible to communicate. . . .
Real communication can only take
　　place where there is silence.
　　　—JIDDU KRISHNAMURTI (1895–1986),
　　　INDIAN EDUCATOR AND PHILOSOPHER

Listening carefully demonstrates respect for the ideas and thoughts of others. Senge and colleagues (1994) describe this intense listening as "the art of developing deeper silences in yourself, so you can slow your mind's hearing to your ears' natural speed and hear beneath the words to their meaning" (p. 377). Listening carefully requires the purposeful pursuit of meaning beneath the words—listening for the contribution in each other's speaking rather than for the assessment or judgment of what is being said. This deeper level of listening asks listeners to set their thoughts aside while they attempt to understand the message from the speaker's point of view. Here are some activities that can help groups examine their listening skills.

Say Something About It. This activity provides participants some insights into their listening. A leader brings an interesting object to the circle of participants. As the participants pass the object around the circle, each person says something about the object. Typically, the participants will be thinking about what they are going to say rather than listening to the comments of others. As the object continues to be passed, a shift often occurs when the comments begin building on one another. For example, if a pencil were going around the circle, initial comments might be "It's yellow," "It's made of wood," or "You write with it." After a while, related comments begin to emerge, such as "I will write Emma a letter with the pencil," and "I will address the envelope using the pencil." This shift shows that the group is beginning to listen and think as a team rather than as individuals.

What's on My Mind? A leader divides the group into pairs and gives one person, the speaker, a topic to speak on. The speaker has five minutes to talk about the topic without deviating. The other person is the listener, but he is listening to the thoughts going through his head. The listener must say those thoughts out loud as the speaker is talking about the topic. This very noisy activity confirms for participants that a large percentage of their brain is not focused on listening but is busy having other thoughts.

Appreciative Partner Statements. This activity reaffirms the difficulty of listening, especially when the topic is *you*. It is done in pairs. One person makes an appreciative statement to the other person and then vice versa, moving back and forth for three to five minutes. No comments on the statements are permitted. Partners are inclined to comment on the statement with a defensive response: "Oh, I really didn't do that" or "It wasn't that much

work." The trick is to control your "automatic" responses so you can listen and receive the acknowledgment, yet not comment on it.

Instrumental in establishing a culture of respect and trust, careful listening sends a message that each idea from each individual brings value to the group conversation—that the group treats each idea with respect, regardless of agreement or disagreement. Senge and colleagues (1994), in *The Fifth Discipline Fieldbook*, suggest some guidelines for listening carefully (see box, "Strategies for Listening Carefully").

Strategies for Listening Carefully

- Stop talking both to others and yourself! Learn to quiet the voice within.
- Try to imagine the other person's viewpoint.
- Show honest, intent interest in the speaker.
- Consider nonverbal behavior to aid in establishing meaning beyond what is spoken.
- Listen for implicit as well as explicit meanings. Question your interpretations of those meanings.
- Speak affirmatively while listening. Avoid evaluative, critical, or disparaging comments at the time the message is being sent.
- Rephrase what the speaker has told you periodically to ensure your understanding of the message.
- Remember to stop talking because all techniques for deep and careful listening depend on this silence (Senge et al., 1994, p. 391).

Share Relevant Information

Information is the material of learning. Group members bring a depth and diversity of information to group conversations. Groups greatly benefit from this wealth of information, especially when the expectation is that all information relevant to the topic is publicly shared. Barriers exist to sharing information among team members. Feelings of inferiority or lack of status may create a reluctance to share information with the group. Members may be shy, reluctant to speak in public, or assume that everybody knows what they know. Others may refuse to make the effort to effectively share relevant information, or they may have controversial information that they are afraid to share (Lumsden & Lumsden, 1993; Weiss, 1994).

Sharing relevant information means offering ideas that contribute to the group discussion even when they do not support a personal idea or perspective. For example, a staff member may want to attend a professional development conference on the day her team has planned a field trip. If she shares this, the team may encourage her not to go to the conference. Sharing all relevant information means telling the team about the conflict, even though the information may reduce her chance of being able to go to the conference. The voicing of multiple perspectives is a good indicator that group members are sharing all relevant information.

Information is valuable only if all group members share and understand it. Information may be sabotaged if people use language such as, "I may be wrong but. . . ." In this example, the group's attention is likely to be diverted to evaluating the information, rather than listening to it. Feelings are also relevant information to share. Feelings may be about the topic under discussion or about the way a topic is being discussed.

Develop Shared Meaning

> Shared meaning is really the cement that holds society together and you could say that the present society has some very poor quality cement. If you make a building with very low quality cement, it cracks and falls apart. We really need the right cement, the right glue . . . and that is shared meaning (Bohm, 1990, p. 17).

A lack of shared meaning is a primary reason for failed communication in groups. This lack of shared meaning can relate to words and ideas, as well as to the purpose and tasks of a group. The need to come to agreement on the meaning of words is an ongoing process in collaborative learning groups. Because we, as speakers, are perfectly clear about what our words and ideas mean, we often assume other group members have the same clarity. We forge ahead making our point rather than pausing for a moment to check for understanding. Unfortunately, the entire group does not necessarily have the same understandings.

For example, I might say I am interested in creating quality instructional programs. I have a clear image of what quality means, but the other group members might not share that image. Quality may look totally different to them. If we don't pause to explore what quality means to each person, we have no guarantee we are advocating for the same goal.

There are several ways to encourage creating shared meaning. One way is to slow down the conversation so individuals have time to explore meanings. Several strategies may help slow down the pace of a conversation (see box, "Strategies for Developing Shared Meaning").

Strategies for Developing Shared Meaning

• Asking for clarification of an idea or word.
• Asking other members to paraphrase the idea that was just expressed.
• Asking group members to discuss the pros and cons of an idea.
• Stopping and defining the word or idea when it first enters the discussion.

For example, when a group was discussing the idea of *consensus*, one team member offered this definition for the group to consider: "We are talking about making our decisions using 'consensus.' To me consensus means unanimous agreement and not majority agreement. Is that what it means to you?" (Schwarz, 1994)

Another way to create shared meaning is to use the four-step process adapted from the work of Russo and Giblin (1996, p. T-2).

Step 1. Each team member offers an interpretation of the task or concept.

Step 2. Team members question each other's ideas.

Step 3. Team members modify their ideas.

Step 4. Team members agree on a shared meaning of the task or concept.

Make Assumptions Explicit

A teacher approaches a colleague to talk about a student with a behavior problem. The colleague listens and then offers several suggestions. The teacher is quick with a response: "I've tried the first one before. It didn't work, and the other one is just not my style." This response left the colleague feeling judged and cut off. What happened? The teacher described a problem. The colleague suggested solutions. The teacher rejected the solutions.

This conversation was solution driven: the participants were addressing a crisis or problem. The teachers gave their attention only to potential solutions, not to the assumptions associated with the problem. Conversations that are held at the "what-should-we-do" level tend to look like a ping-pong game, with answers being batted back and forth. What is missing in a solution-driven conversation is the opportunity to examine the thoughts or the assumptions that created the problem.

Every problem is based on a set of assumptions. Assumptions are ideas that are treated like "the truth," but in reality they are merely *ideas*, created by people at some point in time. In our example, the student's behavior was a problem. The problem is based on a set of assumptions about appropriate ways to behave in school. A different teacher might embrace a different set of assumptions, and the student's behavior might not be a problem in that class. Once team members identify and state underlying assumptions, the team can more easily determine discrepancies in thinking among team members.

Making assumptions explicit is akin to the notion of "suspending assumptions" found in dialogue. Dialogue is a method of discourse "in which group members seek to understand one another's viewpoints and deeply held assumptions" (Garmston & Wellman, 1998, p. 31). As groups engage in dialogue, members are encouraged to identify and "suspend" their assumptions. In this context, *suspend* does not mean to hold back or temporarily dismiss assumptions, but rather it means to *hold them out in front,* like an object, so all can see them clearly. Senge (1990) suggests that individuals have their assumptions " 'hanging in front,' constantly accessible to questioning and observation" (p. 243).

When people are engaged in collaborative learning, examining the thinking behind their ideas can help illuminate underlying assumptions (see box, "Strategies for Making Assumptions Explicit").

Inquiring into the thinking of others can also illuminate assumptions. When inquiring, the listener asks for clarification to more fully understand the speaker's thoughts. In collaborative learning, a clear understanding of the speaker's point of view should precede the voicing of agreement, disagreement, or another point of view. This idea resonates with Covey's (1989) thinking in *The Seven Habits of Highly Effective People,* "Seek first to understand . . . then to be understood" (p. 235). Tool 7, "Left-Hand Column," in Part III, "Tools for Learning," is designed to help individuals and groups identify and discuss underlying assumptions and beliefs.

Decide by Consensus

In this book, we focus on creating a space and process in which teams are free to engage in collaborative learning—free to explore, inquire, expand, and experiment. Although most of these words are open-ended, ignoring the need for teams to make decisions, reach agreement, and take action would be foolish. Every team needs an agreed-on decision-making process. We propose consensus as the optimal decision-making process for collaborative learning teams.

Making decisions by consensus means that

> everyone in the group freely agrees with the decision and will support it. If even one person cannot agree with a proposed decision, the group does not have a consensus. Consensus ensures that team members' choices will be free . . . and that they will be internally committed to the choices (Schwarz, 1994, p. 84).

When a teams uses the consensus process, the group more fully owns the final decision, thereby fostering a more accepting atmosphere for the change.

Power among group members is equalized when consensus is used as a decision-making process because all members must speak their

---

Strategies for Making Assumptions Explicit

1. Telling others the reasons for doing or suggesting something.
2. Explaining the way a certain point of view came to be.
3. Describing the theory on which a strategy is based.

concerns and express their support for a decision. In a group situation it often takes courage to state one's views and inquire more deeply into the thoughts of others. The effective use of the other communication norms such as listening carefully, sharing relevant information, developing shared understanding, and making assumptions explicit increases the likelihood that a group will reach consensus amicably and in a timely manner.

Testing for consensus is often necessary to determine if a group is nearing consensus. Judy Olson-Ness (1994) suggests several ways to determine this point (see box, "Strategies to Test for Consensus").

Strategies to Test for Consensus

• Look at each person individually and ask, "Will you support this decision?"
• Use the five-to-fist test for agreement, with five meaning "yes" and fist meaning "no."
• Have each person place a marker on a consensus continuum chart.
• Ask each member's opinion in a round robin.

Optimal times to test for consensus are as follows:

• The discussion has gone on for a long time.
• Ideas are being repeated.
• Confusion exists about the direction of the discussion.
• Time is running out.
• Options need to be eliminated.

Schwarz (1994) offers a procedure for reaching consensus:

> When a group thinks it is close to reaching consensus, one member should state the decision under consideration, and then each member should say whether he or she agrees. This avoids the mistake of assuming that silence means agreement (p. 84).

Tool 8, "The Pyramid," in Part III, "Tools for Learning," is a method to help groups find common ground and reach consensus—first by pairs, then in groups of 4, then 8, then 16, and so on until the group reaches consensus.

Group Practices That Support Collaborative Learning

Establish Ground Rules

Ground rules are specific and concrete rules and procedures that guide the way collaborative learning groups function. Ground rules provide parameters for team meeting functions, such as scheduling, attendance, agenda development, and members' roles and responsibilities. Ground rules may specify behavioral expectations, such as respecting individual contributions and full participation of all team members. They may delineate procedures for group processes, such as brainstorming, decision making, or recruiting new members.

Having teams generate their own ground rules provides the opportunity to discuss and make explicit the expectations members have for one another. Stress often builds among team members around interpersonal behaviors or "pet peeves," such as the person who is constantly late, the member who dominates the conversation, or the phone calls that continually interrupt the flow of conversation. When teams clearly articulate their ground rules and give responsibility to the group members to enforce them, team members find they function with less stress and greater productivity. "Ground Rules," Tool 9 in Part III, "Tools for Learning," offers a process for groups to discuss and identify relevant and meaningful ground rules (see also Figure 6.1).

FIGURE 6.1
Sample Ground Rules for Meetings

1. Start and end on time.
2. Stay on the task—avoid side conversations or other work.
3. Minimize interruptions—take messages and make phone calls at breaks.
4. Allow everyone an equal voice.
5. Listen to increase your understanding, rather than to think about what you want to say next.
6. Honor promises and commitments made. Follow through on action plans.
7. Be aware, and monitor how much air space you and others are using. Notice patterns (Bailey, 1995).

Some group processes, such as brainstorming, problem solving, or decision making, also need ground rules or procedures that everyone can agree on. Figure 6.2 shows a sample of brainstorming ground rules.

Explore Trust and Task Roles

We began this chapter by emphasizing the importance of trust within a group. Trust is half of what it takes to be an effective and efficient group. The other half is the ability to

accomplish the task. Researchers have identified roles that enhance the levels of trust and task completion in a group. For example, *summarizing* is a task role that is responsible for clearly restating what the group has discussed, and *gatekeeping* is a trust role that makes sure all group members have an opportunity to share their ideas. Figures 6.3 and 6.4 delineate some task and trust roles, respectively (Johnson & Johnson, 1994; Olson-Ness, 1994).

Having team members focus on both trust and task roles has several benefits. Two obvious benefits are a higher level of trust and performance among group members. A less obvious benefit is a leveling of the hierarchical structure inherent in the roles of parent, teacher, administrator, and assistant teacher. This hierarchy is often unconsciously transferred to the collaborative learning situation. By assigning members the roles of summarizer, gatekeeper, or recorder, a message is sent that all members are equally important to the group's functioning. When a group is first "trying on" trust and task roles, members may decide to blindly choose the roles at the beginning of a meeting, or they may select roles that represent their personal style and comfort level.

FIGURE 6.2
Sample Ground Rules
for Brainstorming

1. Share ideas in a round-robin fashion.
2. Avoid negative or judgmental comments.
3. Welcome wild ideas.
4. Focus on quantity, not quality.
5. Keep the sessions short—three to five minutes.
6. Designate a recorder to write key phrases.

FIGURE 6.3 Task Roles That Support Group Functioning	
Information or opinion seeker	Requests facts, seeks relevant information, asks for suggestions and ideas
Recorder	Charts relevant information during meeting, restates group comments or decisions to ensure understanding and agreement
Timekeeper	Ensures each agenda item has a set time; keeps group apprised of time (gives 5-minute warning); when 1 minute is left, asks group members if they want to allot more time to discussion or summarize and move on
Facilitator	Helps group set the agenda, assigns roles for meeting, keeps discussion on topic, reminds group of ground rules and norms, creates the space for action to occur in the meeting
Summarizer	Restates what the group has discussed, pulls together related ideas or suggestions, organizes ideas so group will know what has been said, checks for understanding and agreement

Document Information

Groups that generate information need to document it. Meeting agendas and meeting notes (1) provide a record of topics addressed, decisions made, and assigned responsibilities; and (2) serve as an information dissemination mechanism for people who could not attend the meeting.

There are many methods of keeping meeting notes. One is to keep a running record of the discussions and decisions and then type and distribute the information. Having a laptop computer at the meeting has made this approach more efficient. A more succinct method is to record only group decisions, individual responsibilities, and due dates. During the meeting, it is helpful if decisions are recorded on chart paper so all members can see the decisions and review them before the meeting is adjourned. A "recorder" can then type the chart paper notes and distribute them to each member after the meeting (see Figure 6.5

for a form that makes it easy to take notes on a meeting's agenda items).

Reflect on Group Process

Learning how to learn together is essential to the work of collaborative learning groups. Often, teams pay too much attention to *what* group members are doing, rather than to *how* they are doing it. As stated earlier in this chapter, the balance between trust and task, between focusing on relationships and on accomplishments, is key to successful group functioning. The probability that a team will work on the same task again is minimal. The probability that the team will work collaboratively again is much greater. Therefore, *teams must continually evaluate and refine how they communicate, how they run meetings, how they share information—how they function as a team.*

Group reflection is a means for group members to examine what they are doing well and

71

FIGURE 6.4 Trust Roles That Support Group Functioning	
Gatekeeper	Ensures that all members of the group have an opportunity to share, asks for the opinion of quiet group members, encourages talkative members to be listeners, keeps communication flowing
Encourager	Is friendly, warm, and responsive to others; accepts and acknowledges the contribution of members; encourages others to speak
Compromiser	In the case of an impasse, clearly states the different ideas that have been expressed and asks group to look for common ground; offers compromises for opposing points of view; is willing to yield when it is necessary for progress to be made
Reflector	Senses feelings, moods, and relationships within group; shares own feelings with the group

what needs to be improved, and to set priorities for enhancing their collaborative learning.

Groups can improve their ability to function as a group by setting aside time at each meeting to critique their behavior. Schwarz (1994) suggests several questions for group members to ask themselves (see box, "Questions for Group Reflection").

A similar inquiry can be made into the group's use of communication norms. "Communication Patterns," Tool 10 in Part III, "Tools for Learning," is a way to record and share group communication patterns during team meetings. An observer diagrams the communication patterns that occur over time and presents the data to the group. Discussion about the flow of communication within the group can significantly contribute to positive team functioning.

Another method of ascertaining the members' level of satisfaction with team functioning is through the "Team Functioning Scale" (Figure 6.6), a simple tabulation procedure. The "Why?" column offers information about the forces that are supporting or inhibiting the group's performance. The recorder can include team comments in the meeting notes, and the team can review the comments at the beginning of the next meeting to reinforce the group learning process.

☛ ☛ ☛

In this book, we are asking a lot of educators. In urging staff members to choose collaborative learning as a vehicle for school

Questions for Group Reflection

1. What ground rules did we use well?
2. What ground rules do we need to improve on?
3. Exactly what will we do differently next time?

FIGURE 6.5
Sample Meeting Agenda Notes

Meeting Date: Facilitator:
Members Present: Recorder:
                                                 Timekeeper:

Agenda Item	Time	Decisions	Who	When

Next Group Meeting Date, Time, and Place:

Agenda Items:

Reflection on Group Functioning:

FIGURE 6.6
Team Functioning Scale

Scale	Tallies	Why?
7	/ I'm very satisfied with our team's functioning.	
6	///	
5	/	
4	//	
3	/	
2		
1	I'm very dissatisfied with our team's functioning.	

improvement, we ask them to take a giant step away from business as usual. We are asking that they devote time and energy to understand their own beliefs and the beliefs of those around them. We are asking that they engage in meaningful learning as a team. We are asking that they recognize and address the complexities that accompany working collaboratively. These are not simple requests. They involve time, study, and a commitment to improving the way adults relate to each other in a school.

Yet it is becoming more and more apparent that professional collaboration plays a significant role in quality schools. For that reason, we must persist in exploring new and improved ways for professionals in our schools to grow and learn together. Now is the time to pave the way for "best practice" in collaborative learning. In the next generation of schools, we must be as attentive to the process of learning together as we are to the content of our professional learning.

III

Tools for Learning

Part III presents 10 tools that are relevant to building professional learning communities. Many are multipurpose tools that educators can modify according to the needs of the group. For example, Tool 1, "Force Field Analysis," helps groups identify both negative and positive aspects of an issue being discussed; Tool 4, "Open Space," helps group members find common interests and questions; and Tool 5, "Think, Pair, Share," allows group members to reflect on and share ideas in a preliminary fashion. The description of each tool includes its purpose, step-by-step directions, and tips for debriefing and adapting the process.

Tools for Learning

The tools described in this section are useful activities for developing professional learning communities. These activities are more complex than those outlined in previous chapters and go into more detail. Many require some debriefing, either during or following the activity, and benefit from the use of an experienced facilitator. Several activities are basic process tools that many groups can use throughout the collaborative learning experience. Each tool includes a reference to one or more chapters of this book and sources included in the references.

Each tool outlines the purpose, the basics, the process, and facilitator's notes. Although we have provided some examples and suggestions for adaptations, you may want to adapt the tools further to meet the specific learning needs of your audience. For example, you can use small-group activities requiring discussion with large audiences by asking participants to discuss the concept or issue with their neighbors. The outcomes may not be exactly the same, but participants have still had the opportunity to discuss issues. We encourage you to use these tools as a starting point and to contribute your own personal creativity and individual touches to enhance them.

TOOL 1 | Force Field Analysis

SEE CHAPTER 4

PURPOSE

To identify negative and positive forces that influence the issue being discussed and begin to generate a strategy or plan of action.

This process could be used by

☞ A whole school community to identify the positive or negative forces that affect movement toward its desired state.

☞ A collaborative learning team to analyze positive and negative forces affecting a topic of study.

BASICS

NUMBER OF PARTICIPANTS: Large or small group
TIME NEEDED: 30 minutes to 1 hour
ROOM ARRANGEMENT: Participants should be able to read chart or overhead.
MATERIALS: Overhead or large chart; markers

PROCESS

1. The group identifies desired state and describes it at the top of the chart (See example.)
2. The group develops a list of *facilitating* (positive) forces, including individual, inter-personal, school, and societal forces, that will help the group move toward the desired state. The group addresses this question: What forces existing both within the school/group and outside of the group will help to make the needed changes?
3. The group develops a list of *restraining* (negative) forces that may prohibit the group from moving toward the desired state. The group addresses this question: What forces will prevent change from occurring?
4. The group ranks the facilitating forces according to the degree of influence they have on movement toward the desired state.

CONTINUED

TOOL 1 | Force Field Analysis

SEE CHAPTER 4

5. The group rates the top restraining forces according to how easily they can be resolved (number one being most easily resolved). Identify only the forces that the group can influence given their current resources. (See second "Facilitator's Note.")

6. The group brainstorms ways to strengthen and enhance the top facilitating forces.

7. The group brainstorms ways to convert the restraining forces into facilitating or neutral forces.

EXAMPLE

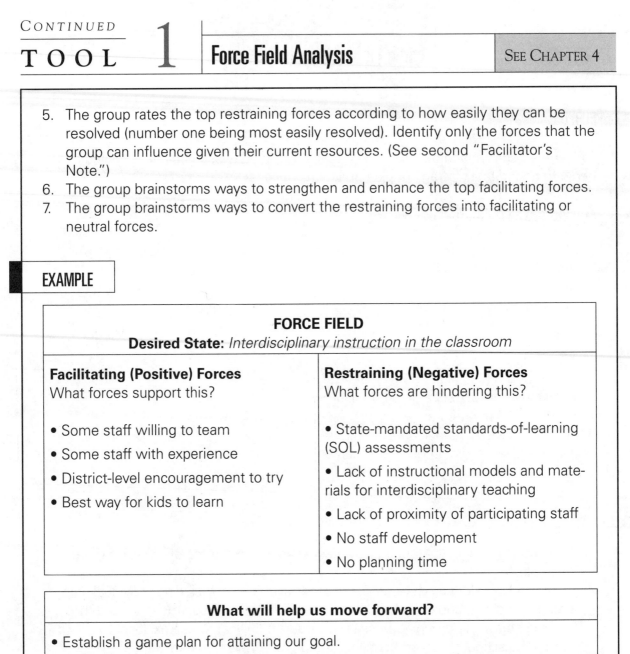

FORCE FIELD

Desired State: *Interdisciplinary instruction in the classroom*

Facilitating (Positive) Forces What forces support this?	Restraining (Negative) Forces What forces are hindering this?
• Some staff willing to team • Some staff with experience • District-level encouragement to try • Best way for kids to learn	• State-mandated standards-of-learning (SOL) assessments • Lack of instructional models and materials for interdisciplinary teaching • Lack of proximity of participating staff • No staff development • No planning time

What will help us move forward?

• Establish a game plan for attaining our goal.

• Talk with principal about logistical matters, such as planning time, staff development, proximity, and materials.

• Visit with staff in schools that have done interdisciplinary instruction at our grade level—see if they would be willing to mentor us.

See Chapter 4

CONTINUED

T O O L 1 | **Force Field Analysis**

FACILITATOR'S NOTES

☛ Johnson and Johnson (1994) claim that reducing the restraining forces is usually a more effective strategy than enhancing the positive or facilitating forces.

☛ Stephen Covey's (1989) discussion of the "circle of influence" and the "circle of concern" in *Seven Habits of Highly Effective People* is applicable in the ranking and action-plan stages of force field analysis. Covey suggests that groups first work on items that are within the circle of influence—that is, items that they can change given the current resources. He believes that *focusing on things that can be improved* will support the change effort. Over time the circle of influence will increase. Conversely, he believes that spending time on issues that cannot be changed leads to frustration and impotence. We recommend that the facilitator help the group target forces it can influence.

Sources: Covey (1989); Johnson and Johnson (1994).

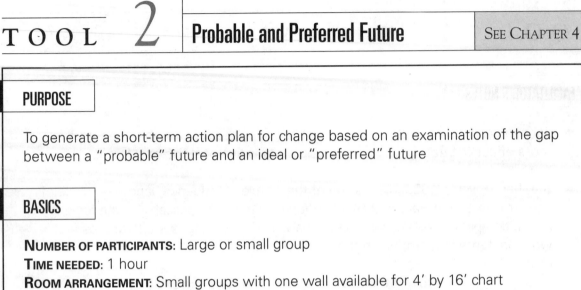

TOOL 2 — Probable and Preferred Future

SEE CHAPTER 4

PURPOSE

To generate a short-term action plan for change based on an examination of the gap between a "probable" future and an ideal or "preferred" future

BASICS

NUMBER OF PARTICIPANTS: Large or small group
TIME NEEDED: 1 hour
ROOM ARRANGEMENT: Small groups with one wall available for 4' by 16' chart
MATERIALS: Roll of chart paper at least 4' by 16'; markers and tape

PROCESS

1. The facilitator prepares a chart with three columns: "Probable Future," "Preferred Future," and "Action Plan for Change" (see example).

2. The facilitator asks staff members: "Think about the current state of education in your school, your state, and the nation. If the current trends continue, what is the probable future scenario for your school?" Staff first generate their own ideas about the probable future and then work in small groups to collect and refine ideas. Main ideas are then reported to the group and listed in the "Probable Future" column on the chart.

3. The facilitator asks staff to brainstorm what they would prefer to have happen in their school. Again, individuals first generate their own list of images for their preferred future and then discuss and refine the list in small groups. The facilitator then lists main ideas in the "Preferred Future" column.

4. Based on the information in the two columns, the next activity is to generate actions that individuals and the group can take to move the school toward its preferred future. Small groups discuss possible actions for change and then pose ideas to the large group. The facilitator records ideas in the "Action Plan for Change" column.

CONTINUED

TOOL *2* | **Probable and Preferred Future** | SEE CHAPTER 4

EXAMPLE

Probable Future	Preferred Future	Action Plan for Change (Implications for the next 6 months)
• Increased use of alternative schooling: charters, vouchers, home schooling • Decline in confidence in public schools • Funding decreased, no bonds passed • Greater gap in school's ability to meet the needs of children and families	• Learning environments in schools that are healthy, safe, and exciting; shared responsibility between home and school • Community dialogue about school reform with active, informed, involved citizenry • Increasing interest from corporations for public school support • Technology supports for individualized student work • Increased accountability for parents, students, and teachers to accomplish stated outcomes	**As individuals** • Begin to collect research on schools with successful reforms (Allison and Myra) • Collect information on our current programs that are successful (Laura) • Talk to community individuals about needed school changes (pairs of staff members to interview identified community stakeholders) **As a group** • Continue rehashing and refining these ideas • Complete assessment of technology capability

CONTINUED

TOOL *2* | **Probable and Preferred Future** | SEE CHAPTER 4

FACILITATOR'S NOTES

☛ After generating items for the "Preferred Future" column, staff may need time to discuss any ideas that are unclear, are controversial, or have only minimum support. If opinions about the school's direction for a preferred future differ, the facilitator helps groups identify ideas that have a common base of support. One way to identify ideas that have general support is to give participants two to four dot stickers and have them put dots by the ideas that they feel are most important. The action plan for change is then based on the most-supported ideas. Completing the "Probable and Preferred Future" template marks the beginning of the action plan process. After the group suggests possible action plans for change, the group must agree to specific actions that they are committed to and have the most leverage for effecting change. Once the group selects these actions, they distribute specific responsibilities among group members.

☛ Establishing an "Action Plan for Change" may be a long process and can be scheduled at a later date, allowing participants time to process the discrepancy between the way things are currently and their preferred future. If this process takes two sessions to complete, it is helpful to hang the partially completed chart in the staff lounge to promote further thought and discussion.

Source: Bailey (1995).

T O O L *3* | Affinity

SEE CHAPTERS 4, 5, AND 6

PURPOSE

To group or cluster similar ideas

BASICS

NUMBER OF PARTICIPANTS: Large or small group
TIME NEEDED: 1 hour (varies depending on size of group)
ROOM ARRANGEMENT: Room with at least one blank wall that can be used to post ideas; movable chairs; tables, optional
MATERIALS: Post-it notes and pens for all participants

PROCESS

1. Each participant writes on Post-it notes ideas pertaining to the topic being discussed (one Post-it for each idea).

2. In a round-robin fashion, each participant shares her idea with the group and places the Post-it on the wall.

3. As participants continue to share their ideas, they cluster similar ideas together.

4. The group gives a name, title, or category to each "cluster" of ideas.

FACILITATOR'S NOTES

☛ This tool is an expedient method for clustering the ideas of individual group members. For example, when defining schoolwide professional development goals in an inclusive school, a facilitator asked staff members: "How do you need to stretch to increase your capacity to collaboratively offer quality programs for all children in inclusive classrooms?" Responses generated clusters such as facilitating peer interaction, teaching children with challenging behaviors, team teaching, and differentiating instruction. The group then translated these areas into school-based professional development goals.

MACEL

CONTINUED

TOOL 3 | Affinity | SEE CHAPTERS 4, 5, AND 6

☛ The "Affinity" exercise can also be used to

– form collaborative learning teams based on individual learning interests.

– generate a plan for exploring the team's topic of study that honors the needs and interests of the individuals. (For example, who learns best through reading, site visits, consultants, peer coaching, and so forth?)

– identify similar and dissimilar views of a topic being discussed, such as beliefs about how young children learn.

☛ The facilitator can conduct this tool "en masse," where a group moves to the "posting wall" and posts ideas without first reading the idea to the entire group. Participants are encouraged to individually read the ideas that have already been posted; actively discuss their ideas and the ideas of others as they post; and begin to create clusters of ideas, putting similar ideas together. When the sorting is done, the facilitator reads aloud idea clusters so the group can generate names for the clusters.

☛ This process can also be done in silence. Participants move to the posting wall, post their ideas, and rearrange ideas into clusters without talking. The absence of talking focuses the group on reading and thinking.

☛ When working in small groups, a tabletop is a good surface for posting and clustering ideas. For best results, the table should be cleared, with participants sitting evenly spaced around the table.

☛ When clusters are read aloud, additional ideas may be generated and added to a cluster, or individuals may decide that an idea belongs in a different cluster.

T O O L  | Open Space

SEE CHAPTERS 4 AND 5

PURPOSE

To assist staff members in (1) identifying a personally meaningful topic for study and (2) forming study groups with staff who share similar interests and questions

BASICS

NUMBER OF PARTICIPANTS: Large group, 20–50 people
TIME NEEDED: 1 hour
ROOM ARRANGEMENT: Large open room; movable chairs; space on at least three walls for charts
MATERIALS: Chart paper, pens

PROCESS

1. Room preparation: A large open room is divided into stations with one schoolwide professional development goal posted at each station. The facilitator posts the goals on a long strip of paper with four pieces of chart paper mounted side by side below (see example). The charts are titled as follows:

    - The Stroll: Interests/concerns
    - First Round of Discussion
    - Second Round of Discussion
    - Topics for Study

CONTINUED

T O O L   4 | **Open Space** | SEE CHAPTERS 4 AND 5

EXAMPLE

The Wall

Goal: Provide individualized instruction for all children in school

(chart)	(chart)	(chart)	(chart)
The Stroll: Interests/ Concerns	**First Round of Discussion**	**Second Round of Discussion**	**Topics for Study**

1. When the group assembles, the facilitator reviews the entire "Open Space" process. The facilitator explains the use of charts and transition cues and demonstrates their use, if appropriate.

2. *The Stroll (20 minutes):* Individuals randomly circulate to each station in the room and record on "The Stroll" chart their personal interests and concerns about each professional development goal. For example, with the goal "Improve coteaching skills," one teacher might write, "Learn efficient planning strategies" on the chart; and another might write, "Learn more about models of coteaching." Teachers are encouraged to add personal ideas to all the goals. After 15 minutes, the facilitator shows the 5-minute warning sign. That is the cue for participants to review the material on all the charts and move to the station that best captures their learning interest.

CONTINUED

T O O L 4 | Open Space

SEE CHAPTERS 4 AND 5

3. *First Round of Discussion (15 minutes):* Using movable chairs, participants cluster in discussion circles at the station that most interests them. Participants share their reason for selecting this station and the things they want to learn about this goal. A recorder notes each person's interests on the "First Round of Discussion" chart. The group then reflects on what it has heard and whether a specific topic for study has emerged. Any study ideas that emerge from the discussion are posted on the "Topics for Study" chart.

4. *Second Round of Discussion (10 minutes):* This is an opportunity for individuals to explore a second area of interest. For the second round of discussion, participants move to a new station, review the work of the previous discussion group, and repeat the discussion process outlined in Step 3. Ideas are recorded on the "Second Round of Discussion" chart. New ideas emerging from this group are added to the "Topics for Study" chart.

5. *Topics for Study:* Individuals move to the station with the professional development goal that most interests them. This is the first step in forming a collaborative learning team. When staff have grouped themselves into learning teams, they note their broad topic for study on chart paper, as well as the team members' names and their personal interests related to the topic. The facilitator and group representatives then share these charts with the entire staff.

FACILITATOR'S NOTES

☞ Identifying schoolwide professionals development goals precedes the "Open Space" exercise. These goals, generated by the entire staff, reflect areas in which staff need to grow to attain school vision.

☞ It is helpful to have a facilitator for each of the topic groups. If a facilitator is not available, an individual from each group should assume the role of facilitator to keep the discussion focused, be sure all ideas are expressed, and document the discussion.

☞ During the first and second rounds of discussion, the facilitator may want to begin with an open-ended question, such as, "Why does this topic interest you?"

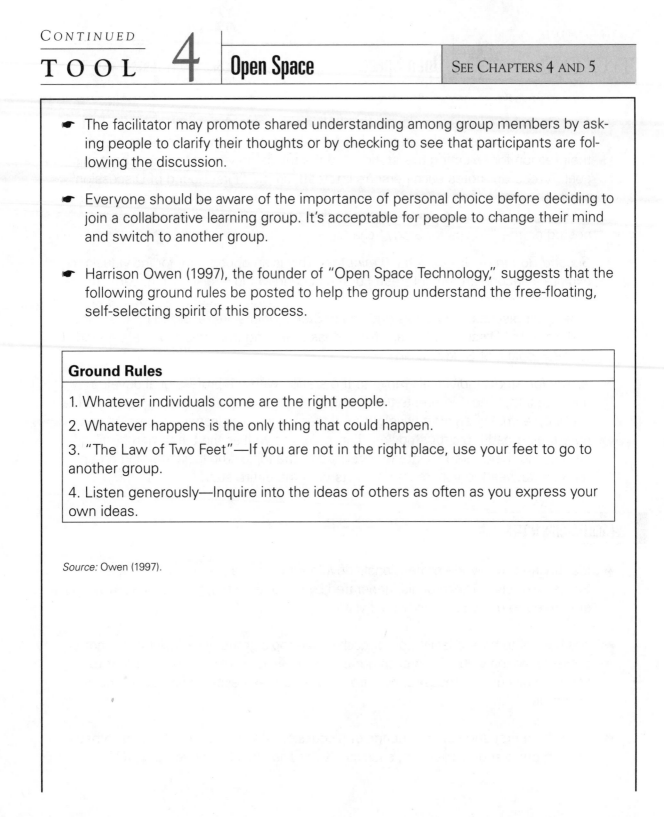

CONTINUED

T O O L 4 | Open Space SEE CHAPTERS 4 AND 5

☞ The facilitator may promote shared understanding among group members by asking people to clarify their thoughts or by checking to see that participants are following the discussion.

☞ Everyone should be aware of the importance of personal choice before deciding to join a collaborative learning group. It's acceptable for people to change their mind and switch to another group.

☞ Harrison Owen (1997), the founder of "Open Space Technology," suggests that the following ground rules be posted to help the group understand the free-floating, self-selecting spirit of this process.

Ground Rules
1. Whatever individuals come are the right people.
2. Whatever happens is the only thing that could happen.
3. "The Law of Two Feet"—If you are not in the right place, use your feet to go to another group.
4. Listen generously—Inquire into the ideas of others as often as you express your own ideas.

Source: Owen (1997).

MACK

TOOL 5 | Think, Pair, Share

SEE CHAPTER 5

PURPOSE

To give the participants time to articulate and reflect on their ideas before they present them to a larger group

BASICS

NUMBER OF PARTICIPANTS: Large or small group
TIME NEEDED: 10–20 minutes, depending on group size
ROOM ARRANGEMENT: Seating arrangement that allows two people to talk together
MATERIALS: None

PROCESS

1. At a natural breaking point, the facilitator asks participants to stop and think for a minute about the idea, information, or concept presented.
2. After 1 minute, the facilitator invites participants to turn to someone on their left or right and share their thoughts or ideas. Each partner has 1 minute to share.
3. After 2 minutes of discussion, participants are invited to share ideas, concerns, and questions with the larger group.

FACILITATOR'S NOTES

This process can be used to do the following:

☛ *Identify important points:* The facilitator might say, "What are the two most important points you heard?"

☛ *Analyze the message:* The facilitator might say, "What are you thinking about the speaker's ideas?"

☛ *Develop shared understanding:* The facilitator might say, "What do you believe the speaker is saying?"

☛ *Apply learning:* The facilitator might say, "How might you use this information in your work?"

Source: Garmston and Wellman (1998).

TOOL 6

Communication Norms for Collaborative Groups

SEE CHAPTER 6

PURPOSE

To teach communication norms that promote collaboration*

BASICS

NUMBER OF PARTICIPANTS: Groups of four to seven individuals
TIME NEEDED: 2 hours
ROOM ARRANGEMENT: Tables and chairs for small groups
MATERIALS: "Learning project materials:" role sheets (A–H) and five communication norm sheets

PROCESS

1. *Setup* (5 minutes): The facilitator gives each group (seated around a table) directions for a group learning project. The facilitator assigns a task to each group. For example, the task may be setting up an early childhood environment using wooden blocks of different sizes and colors. The learning project should be open ended, thus challenging the group to develop shared understanding and agreement about their work.

   The facilitator gives role cards (see "Facilitator's Notes") to group members and says, "I have additional information to give to each of you. Please do not share this information with your fellow team members." Role cards distributed have the following roles on them:

   > Withholder (silent but knowing)
   > Always confused
   > Off topic
   > Protector
   > Know-it-all
   > Yes person

---

* Tool 6 is adapted from *Module I: Teams* from *Communication Derailed*, by Eileen Russo, Ph.D., and Chris Giblin. (c) 1996 Organization Design and Development, Inc. Available from HRDQ, 800-633-4533.

2. *Play* (10–15 minutes): The group proceeds to begin work on its project, with group members acting out their specific roles. The facilitator tells teams they have 15 minutes to complete their project and notes comments, body language, and communication flow.

3. *Debrief* (10 minutes): The teams consider the following questions:
   • How were things going?
   • Did you encounter any communication problems?
   The facilitator can address questions to specific people (e.g., "How did you feel, Sue, when Marta continually interrupted you?" "What did you decide?"). The facilitator can contribute observations to stimulate reflection.

4. *Learning* (45 minutes): The groups now look at effective communication norms for teaming and learning. Each of the five norms is described on a separate one-page fact sheet (see "Facilitator's Notes"). Each member of the group takes a norm, reviews it, and prepares to teach it to other group members by completing the activity at the bottom of the sheet. The facilitator can organize cross-team groupings for those individuals who are reviewing the same norm.

   After 10–15 minutes, teams reconvene and each person has 5 minutes to describe his or her norm, help the group practice it, and address questions. After 5 minutes, the facilitator moves the group to the next norm. After the small groups have discussed all norms, the group as a whole takes 5–10 minutes for any large-group discussions.

5. *Replay* (15 minutes): Using the newly learned communication norms, the groups work again to complete their project. The facilitator can coach members, for example, "Remember to develop shared understanding"; can note use of the norms, for example "By repeating what Marta said, you showed you were listening carefully"; or can take notes to provide feedback after the role-play is finished. Communication behaviors might include asking each other questions, actively seeking consensus, actively listening using clarification and paraphrasing, seeking the input of all the members, and checking for shared understanding. The groups get a 5- and 2-minute warning before ending their role-play. The project should be completed in 15 minutes.

6. *Debrief* (15 minutes): The facilitator acknowledges group members for their work at effective communication. The group members pick up materials or move them to the center of the table. Each group shares any product that emerged with the other groups. Each group discusses these questions:

- Did you communicate differently this time?
- What communication norms did you find helpful?
- What communication norms do you want to adopt for your team?

FACILITATOR'S NOTES

☛ If a team has agreed on a set of communication norms, display them in some public way—on a sign or on the agenda page.

☛ To shorten the activity, choose one or two norms to teach during the learning phase.

ROLE CARDS | Communication Norms for Collaborative Groups

Withholder (silent but knowing)

You are an extremely shy person who prefers to work on your own. Unless someone directly asks for your thoughts, you tend not to speak in a group setting. You are aware of the feelings of others around you but are uncomfortable in making any overt attempts to be inclusive or empathetic to other group members. You have knowledge that could assist the group in its task but are uncomfortable in sharing your information. You tend to fidget in your seat, as a sign of your discomfort, but remain a quiet observer.

Always confused

You are a considerate person who desperately wants to contribute to the work of the team. Your mind tends to wander to other issues; thus, you miss a great deal of the conversation. You tend to ask many questions, often disrupting the flow of the discussion to clarify your own thoughts. You often reopen topics that have already been discussed by the group.

CONTINUED

ROLE CARDS | Communication Norms for Collaborative Groups

Yes person

You have your own ideas about the task of the team, yet you tend to go along with the ideas of other members. You contribute to the group but with a focus on getting the task accomplished with as little uneasiness as possible. You tend to smile and agree to the ideas of others—even if their ideas contradict each other.

Protector

You are far more concerned with the feelings of individual group members than you are with the task at hand—to the point that you focus solely on feelings and emotions. You consult individuals who appear to be uncomfortable (fidgeting in their seat, confused) in the middle of a conversation to try to assist them. You take on a parent role in the way you encourage all group members to express their opinion—even if they are not interested in speaking. You often rephrase a harsh statement made by another group member in kinder and gentler words.

CONTINUED

ROLE CARDS | Communication Norms for Collaborative Groups

Know-it-all

You feel very strongly about the direction the activity should take. You are an extremely opinionated person and are often loud and disruptive during a meeting. You are known to interrupt another speaker if you have something you feel is important to say. You feel it is imperative that everyone know your ideas. Your focus is on completing the task at hand in the most expedient manner possible. The feelings and contributions of other members are not important to you.

Off topic

You are excited to see and talk to your colleagues. You are very much a "people person." Spending the day alone in your classroom without other adults to speak with has been frustrating. You take every opportunity in your group meeting to discuss your personal life, children in your class, difficulties you are having with the administration, and other issues with individuals in the group. You are not always aware of the discussion because your mind is focused on personal needs. You continually have side conversations with other team members.

FACT SHEETS | Communication Norms for Collaborative Groups

Listen carefully

Listening carefully demonstrates respect for the ideas and thoughts of others. Peter Senge and colleagues (1994) describe this intense listening as "the art of developing deeper silences in yourself, so you can slow your mind's hearing to your ears' natural speed, and hear beneath the words to their meaning" (p. 377). Listening carefully requires the purposeful pursuit of meaning "beneath the words"—listening for the contribution in each other's speaking rather than assessing or judging what people are saying. This deeper level of listening asks listeners to set their thoughts aside while they attempt to understand the message from the speaker's point of view (see Chapter 6).

Practice:
- Obtain silence: Stop talking to yourself and others.
- Show your interest in what the speaker has to say.
- Try to understand the speaker's point of view.
- Clarify your understanding of the message.
- Question your interpretations.

What are two other techniques you could use to support this norm in your group?

| FACT SHEETS | Communication Norms for Collaborative Groups |

Share relevant information

Sharing relevant information means speaking up if you have ideas and information that will contribute to the group discussion, including facts that do not support your idea or perspective. For example, a staff member may want to attend a professional development conference on the day her team has planned a field trip. If she shares this dilemma, the team may encourage her not to go to the conference. Sharing all relevant information means telling the team about the conflict, even though the information may reduce her chance of being able to go to the conference (see Chapter 6).

Practice:
- Elicit multiple perspectives in the group.
- Share your feelings about the topic.
- Present your information so the message is highlighted, not your feelings about it. For example, if a sentence starts with "This is a stupid idea, but. . .," team member may find themselves contemplating whether they agree or disagree with that statement rather than listening to the information.

What are two other techniques you could use to support this norm in your group?

COMMUNICATION NORMS — CONTINUED

| FACT SHEETS | Communication Norms for Collaborative Groups |

Develop shared meaning

"Shared meaning is really the cement that holds society together" (Bohm, 1990, p. 17). Shared meaning or understanding means that everyone in the group shares the same meaning for words or ideas being discussed by the group. Establishing agreement on the meaning of words is an ongoing process in collaborative learning groups. We often assume that words or ideas expressed over and over in our work or environment hold the same meaning to everyone in the group. For example, one group member might say that he is interested in creating quality instructional programs. The speaker's image of what those programs will look like may not be the same as the image other group members hold. Slowing down the conversation so people have time to explore meanings is necessary for the group to develop a shared understanding of the message (see Chapter 6).

Practice:
- Ask for clarification of an idea or word.
- Ask other members to paraphrase the idea that was just expressed.
- Stop the conversation and define the word or idea under question.

What are two other techniques you could use to support this norm in your group?

| FACT SHEETS | Communication Norms for Collaborative Groups |

Make assumptions explicit

Every problem is based on a set of assumptions. Assumptions are the ideas that are treated like "the truth," but in reality are merely ideas, created by people at some point in time. For example, different teachers may have different sets of assumptions that guide their response to a student's behavior in school. When the assumptions underlying a problem or an idea are identified and clearly stated, discrepancies in thinking among team members can be more easily identified (see Chapter 6).

Practice:
- Ask the speaker to explain how he or she arrived at a particular idea.
- Tell others why you are doing or suggesting something.
- Explain how you came to a certain point of view.
- Describe the theory that you are basing your idea on.

What are two other techniques you could use to support this norm in your group?

COMMUNICATION NORMS — *CONTINUED*

| FACT SHEETS | Communication Norms for Collaborative Groups |

Decide by consensus

Here is a definition of making decisions by consensus:

> Everyone in the group freely agrees with the decision and will support it. If even one person cannot agree with a proposed decision, the group does not have a consensus. Consensus ensures that team members' choices will be free choices and that they will be internally committed to the choices (Schwarz, 1994, p. 84).

When a group uses the consensus process, the group more fully owns the final decision, thereby fostering a more accepting atmosphere for the change. Testing for consensus is important to be sure that a decision is unanimous and to be sure that an individual's silence is not automatically interpreted as agreement (see Chapter 6).

Practice:
- Ask group members individually if they support the decision.
- Take a group vote using thumbs up or thumbs down.

What are two other techniques you could use to support this norm in your group?

Source: Russo and Giblin (1996); Schwarz (1994).

TOOL 7 | Left-Hand Column

SEE CHAPTER 6

PURPOSE

To increase awareness of unspoken assumptions and thoughts during a group discussion and to develop a forum for discussing those assumptions and thoughts with the group

BASICS

NUMBER OF PARTICIPANTS: Two or more; preferably a small group
TIME NEEDED: 10–15 minutes to debrief
ROOM ARRANGEMENT: Comfortable space to write
MATERIALS: A piece of paper divided into two columns for each participant; writing implements

PROCESS

1. Before a team meeting or a small-group discussion, the facilitator gives each participant a "Left-Hand Column" sheet and the following instructions.
   Instructions: The "Left-Hand Column" activity provides individuals with documentation of the topics under discussion (these are listed in the right-hand column), as well as their reactions to the topic being discussed (these are listed in left-hand column).

2. Say to participants:

   "This sheet is for recording information you are hearing and what you think or feel about the information.

   In the *right-hand column,* write the important information that you heard during the group discussion. This column is for factual information—the ideas that everybody hears.

   In the *left-hand column,* write your thoughts or reactions to what people are saying or what is happening during the group discussion. Write what you are thinking and feeling. This column documents your personal thoughts about what is being said. It can include ideas or feelings that have not been

CONTINUED

TOOL **7** | Left-Hand Column | SEE CHAPTER 6

said aloud to the group. This paper is yours to use as a reference in our group discussion. You can choose whether or not to share your thoughts."

Left-Hand Column *Thoughts, Concerns, Opinions*	Right-Hand Column *Information Being Discussed*

3. At an appropriate point during the group discussion, the facilitator asks participants to review their "Left-Hand Column" sheet to see what unspoken factors are influencing their participation in the discussion. Factors may range from considerations about the subject being discussed (agree, disagree) to interpersonal tension (lack of trust, feelings of inadequacy) to physical needs (hungry, cold). All are legitimate issues for group consideration and often point to roadblocks for successful group functioning. The facilitator may pose one or more of the following questions:

   - What were you thinking that you did not say?
   - What were you feeling that you did not say?
   - How are your thoughts influencing your participation in the group discussion?
   - What is an appropriate way to share your thoughts?

4. The facilitator opens a group discussion about issues surfacing in the left-hand column and about the ways this information can be used to improve understanding of group functioning.

CONTINUED

TOOL **7** | **Left-Hand Column** | SEE CHAPTER 6

FACILITATOR'S NOTES

☞ An important point to remember is that no opinion is "right" or "true." Reality, like beauty, is in the eye of the beholder. Within a group, a variety of views always exists. Sometimes members of a group behave as if one opinion or view is right and another is wrong. The original data or the information in the right-hand column is the most objective information available. The left-hand column illuminates the individual interpretations of the objective data. Those interpretations are what is being discussed in the "Left-Hand Column" exercise. The facilitator will want to keep tying what was said with how it was interpreted.

☞ Groups may adapt the "Left-Hand Column" exercise for specific topics to make underlying assumptions more explicit and apparent to the group (see the following example).

Left-Hand Column *Why is that quality an early childhood practice?*	Right-Hand Column *A quality early childhood practice*

☞ On a more interpersonal level, groups may use the exercise to help the listeners distinguish between the speaker's comments and their perceptions of the speaker.

CONTINUED

T O O L   7 | Left-Hand Column   SEE CHAPTER 6

My Thoughts	Speaker's Comments

☛ Here are questions the facilitator may pose for reflection:

   – What was the speaker's intention?
   – Did the speaker achieve his/her intention?
   – What assumptions am I making about the speaker? Why?
   – Did these left-hand column thoughts interfere with communication?

☛ Facilitators should be prepared to share a thought from their left-hand column to get the group started.

Source: Senge (1994).

T O O L 8 | The Pyramid

SEE CHAPTER 6

PURPOSE

To find common ground and reach consensus among members in a group

BASICS

NUMBER OF PARTICIPANTS: Between 8 and 32 people
TIME NEEDED: 20–40 minutes, depending on group size
ROOM ARRANGEMENT: Movable chairs in an open room (no tables)
MATERIALS: Chart paper and markers

our MA·CEI values

PROCESS

This exercise helps group members converge their ideas around a topic, such as values of the community, staff development goals, or beliefs about how young children learn.

1. Participants write down their thoughts or opinions on the topic under discussion.

2. Participants then work in pairs comparing their ideas about the topic. The participants write down the ideas that they have in common or agree on.

3. Two sets of partners combine to make a foursome and repeat the process.

4. Two groups of four combine to make a group of eight and repeat the process.

5. Two groups of 8 combine to make a group of 16 and repeat the process. Groups continue to combine until the whole group is working together to identify common ideas.

CONTINUED

T O O L 8 | The Pyramid

SEE CHAPTER 6

What are our beliefs about how young children learn . . .

Individually . . .

With a partner . . .

Two sets of partners . . .

Two groups of four . . .

Two groups of eight . . .

FACILITATOR'S NOTE

☞ This activity can be used in smaller team meetings with as few as four people and is a useful tool for developing shared meaning.

TOOL 9 | Ground Rules

SEE CHAPTER 6

PURPOSE

To examine and establish ground rules for team functioning

BASICS

NUMBER OF PARTICIPANTS: A team or small group (4–8 people)
TIME NEEDED: 20–40 minutes
ROOM ARRANGEMENT: Chairs arranged so that participants face one another
MATERIALS: Chart paper and markers

PROCESS

1. The facilitator introduces the idea of group rules, using a family as an example:

   "We have all been part of a family. In any family there are certain rules or expectations for what we could or could not do and how we would behave. What were some of the rules or expectations in your family?" (Wait for response.)

   "Most of what we have suggested are rules that helped us work successfully as a family. Just like families, groups or teams in schools have rules or expectations to help the team function smoothly. What are some of the behaviors, both positive and negative, that you have experienced as a team member?" (The facilitator writes thoughts on a "Group Behaviors" chart.)

EXAMPLE

Positive Group Behaviors	Negative Group Behaviors
• Come prepared to the meeting • Be on time • Accept and make no calls during the meeting	• Engage in side conversations • Be chronically late to the meeting • Interrupt the meeting

Mace

CONTINUED

TOOL 9 | Ground Rules

SEE CHAPTER 6

2. The facilitator initiates a group discussion about the messages that the behaviors in each column send to team members.

3. The facilitator leads the group in a discussion about the value in having agreed-on ground rules. After reviewing the sample of possible ground rules, each team or group brainstorms "draft" rules for itself and writes them on a chart. Each team member then gets five dots to put beside the five most important rules. The top-ranked four to six rules become the initial set of ground rules.

Sample Ground Rules

- Start and end on time.

- Participate in no side conversations.

- Minimize interruptions.

- Offer everyone an equal voice.

- Honor promises and commitments.

- Avoid dominating the conversation.

- Listen to understand others.

- Encourage everyone to participate in group work.

- Work from a group-developed agenda.

- Rotate team leadership tasks, such as agenda development, meeting facilitation, and recording.

---

4. After the group identifies four to six top choices, the facilitator seeks consensus to accept these ground rules as expectations for the group. The facilitator is looking for 100 percent agreement. If a group member is unable to commit to a particular rule, the group needs to decide if the rule should be eliminated or if an exception can be made on the basis of the member's situation.

CONTINUED

TOOL 9 | **Ground Rules** | SEE CHAPTER 6

FACILITATOR'S NOTES

☞ Successful teams have clear, well-defined rules by which they operate. Chapter 6 provides a rationale for developing and using team ground rules: "When teams clearly articulate their ground rules and give responsibility to the group members to enforce them, team members find they function with less stress and greater productivity."

☞ Teams often dislike setting rules. They feel it is unnecessary to establish ground rules. To help set the scene for this exercise, ask team members to relate personal stories in which a lack of clarity about expectations led to bad feelings, or in which the lack of ground rules led to the demise of a team.

☞ After the group has identified its ground rules, the facilitator might ask, "Which ground rule, if we could follow it 100 percent, would most improve our teaming?" Teams identify one or two rules and brainstorm strategies to put those rules in place. The facilitator reinforces the implementation of ground rules by scheduling time for feedback at the end of each team meeting.

☞ Establishing rules is only a beginning. Teams should consider the usefulness and effectiveness of their ground rules after each team meeting and revise them as necessary.

T O O L 10 **Communication Patterns** SEE CHAPTER 6

PURPOSE

To increase awareness of group communication patterns and their effect on group functioning

BASICS

NUMBER OF PARTICIPANTS: Maximum 8–10 people
TIME NEEDED: 45 minutes
ROOM ARRANGEMENT: Small discussion groups
MATERIALS: "Patterns of Communication Observer Frequency" Chart

PROCESS

1. A person from each group is chosen to observe the group discussion. The job of the observer is to record the communication patterns within the group and share the recorded data with the group.

2. Before the discussion, the observer creates a diagram of the group's seating arrangement, including the names of each person. Once the discussion begins, the observer makes a tally mark each time a person speaks; and draws an arrow to indicate to whom the person is speaking. When a person is speaking to the whole group, the arrow is drawn to the middle of the diagram. If group members interrupt the flow of the conversation with a negative or off-topic comment, the observer places a minus sign (–) by the person's name. If people offer a supportive statement to other group members, the observer puts a plus sign (+) by their name. Observations are done in 5-minute intervals, with a 5-minute rest between observations. A 30-minute meeting would yield two observations.

TOOL **10** | **Communication Patterns** | SEE CHAPTER 6

5	First 5 minutes	Get diagram ready. Draw circles and label them with participants' names.
10	Second 5 minutes	Observe.
15	Third 5 minutes	Make a second observation chart.
20	Fourth 5 minutes	Observe.
26–30	Last 10 minutes	Transfer data to chart paper to share with group.

3. After about 30 minutes (or a predetermined amount of time), the observer presents the data to the group, and then the facilitator leads a 10- to 15-minute discussion about the data. Potential discussion questions include the following:

• Was this a typical meeting?

• What was the flow of communication within the group—who was speaking to whom?

• What effect did this flow have on the group?

• What changes would you suggest and why?

(See Instructions for sample "Diagram of Communication Patterns" form, p. 115.)

FACILITATOR'S NOTES

☛ This tool uses a process observer who may also be the discussion facilitator. Groups may decide to rotate the process observer role among group members. The process observer records the communication exchanges and then shares the information on the "Patterns of Communication" diagram with the group. The facilitator leads the debriefing discussion.

TOOL 10 | Communication Patterns | SEE CHAPTER 6

☛ Difficult topics may emerge, and the facilitator should be prepared to address issues like these:

- One person speaks all the time.
- One person never speaks.
- Conversation is directed to one person rather than to all members.
- No one encourages the quieter members to speak.

MACEZ –
"Fly on the
Wall"
2nd
Sem

Diagram of Communication Patterns

Observer: _____Sheryl_____   Date: __5/1/99__

Event: _____Team Meeting_____   Time: __8:00 a.m.__

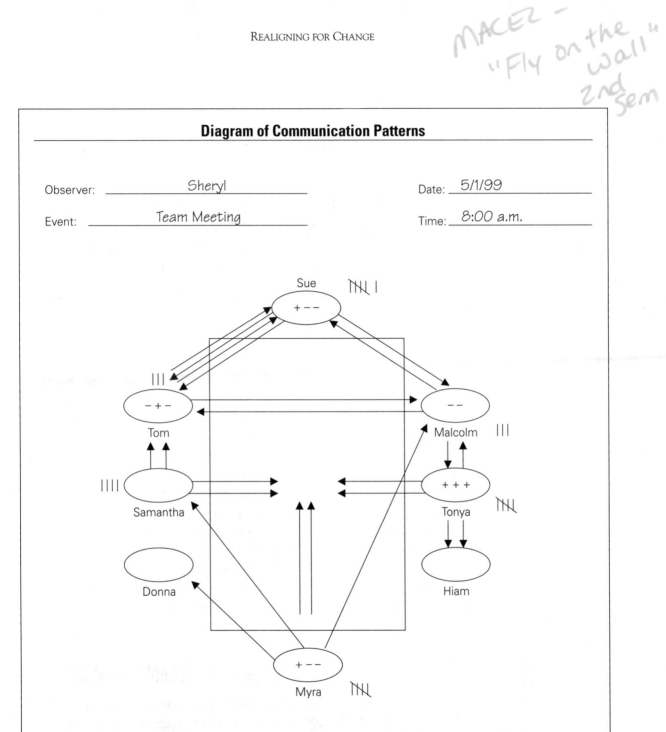

Instructions: Create a diagram of the group's seating arrangement, including the names of each person. Once the discussion begins, make a tally mark each time a person speaks. Draw an arrow to indicate to whom the person is speaking. When a person is speaking to the whole group, draw an arrow to the middle of the diagram. If group members interrupt the flow of the conversation with a negative or off-topic comment, put a minus sign (–) by the person's name. If people offer a supportive statement to other group members, put a plus sign (+) by their name.

Sources: Bailey (1995); Johnson and Johnson (1994).

Epilogue

My experience with Project REALIGN has taught me that two components are present in most successful change initiatives—a strong proactive school leader and a school staff who are committed to learning together and ultimately crafting the initiative to fit the needs of their school community.

—TEACHER AND PROJECT REALIGN FACILITATOR

Having read this book, you may wonder how the REALIGN participants felt about being involved in school-based collaborative learning community. What kind of changes and growth did they report? What helped and hindered the development of their learning communities?

During the REALIGN project period, we piloted the collaborative learning process with approximately 150 participants, including teachers, paraprofessionals, parents, administrators, and specialists, in five public elementary schools. Our research questions examined the effect of collaborative learning on the individuals, on the school community, and on instructional practices. We gathered data from written evaluations, interviews, and focus groups after the first year and, when possible, the second year of intervention at each school.

Individual Change

In looking at individual change, participants reported an increase in professional knowledge and personal confidence, as well as a renewed commitment to lifelong learning. One teacher struck a poetic note when reflecting on her personal growth: "Working in a group will always enlarge your thinking, enrich your being, and excite your mind."

We found that individual growth is reinforced when everyone participates on an equal footing in the learning process. For many parents and paraprofessionals, this project was a novel opportunity to communicate as equals with teachers, therapists, and administrators. An instructional assistant commented: "This experience taught me that I could be more of a leader in my own way and that my opinion matters—it's important, and it counts!"

Change in the School Community

When looking for changes in the school community, participants reported an enhanced ability to work collaboratively and an increased capacity for collective thinking. A new appreciation of roles and responsibilities emerged as general educators, special educators, and other school specialists took time to better understand one another. One teacher commented on the power of this new connectedness:

Much can be accomplished if you approach it with a team attitude, like we did—we're all in this together, and we all want it to happen. If there is a will, there is a way.

Many participants felt that because they had improved their communication skills, their group was more productive and harmonious. One participant stated: "The most important thing to me was learning to listen, to really hear what others were saying, and ask for clarification if needed, not just assuming what I heard was correct."

The collaborative learning process encouraged teams to combine their thoughts to create something bigger than a collection of individual ideas. The value of collective thinking is reflected in this participant's comment:

Supportive teammates shared wonderful ideas, volunteered to do different jobs, assumed different roles, and shared in the decision-making process. The ideas generated by creative minds inspired creativity in others.

Instructional Practices

In the area of instructional practices, teachers reported that their involvement on collaborative learning teams resulted in (1) new tools and strategies for meeting the diverse needs and abilities of their students, (2) enhanced family involvement programs, and (3) increased opportunities for children with and without disabilities to learn together.

Participants often noted a positive correlation between an increased capacity to differentiate instruction and expanded opportunities for the inclusion of children with disabilities in the general education program.

Other Findings

The experience of collaborative learning varied greatly for each individual and each school. As part of the evaluation, we asked participants to identify factors that enhanced or inhibited the building of a collaborative learning culture in their school. Data analysis revealed several reoccurring themes, including time, schoolwide focus, good leadership, and sharing results.

Time

Participants often described time as a double-edged sword. Some said it was difficult to find time, yet they wanted more time to discuss what they were learning. The initial time in planning the learning agenda was often reported as frustrating; with hindsight, however, people frequently changed their opinion. The benefit of collaboration, according to one teacher, is "having the time to work together—a group of people with ownership of a project; the journey of four individuals coming together and finding something to work on as a team and becoming one."

Schoolwide Focus

The evaluation findings highlighted the importance of a schoolwide focus, such as a shared vision, mission, or direction for school improvement. In schools where a strong commitment to a vision was absent, staff had more difficulty in selecting relevant topics for study. Successful schoolwide change required the participation of the entire school staff. Making a difference at the school level was difficult when only part of the staff participated, although many staff members felt it was important to make participation voluntary.

Leadership Style

Participants reported that leadership style and the marshaling of resources to support learning efforts significantly affected the success of this school-based staff development model. The most positive responses came from schools where administrators took active roles on collaborative learning teams. These administrators continually furthered collaborative learning through verbal support and by freeing up time for team meetings. Participants noted that providing resources and aligning the infrastructure to support on-the-job learning were important aspects of the leader's role.

Sharing Results

Finally, the opportunity for the collaborative learning teams to share their findings with their colleagues helped solidify knowledge and spread the newly developed expertise throughout the school. One teacher commented:

> When we presented our information to the whole group, it not only opened it up to us, but we got to show other people what we learned. Then they tried it, and so it crossed over. I think it was really helpful.

Challenges Ahead

A principal in a recent leadership meeting shared this poignant remark: "You are organized to get the results you get." In education today, we don't seem to be getting the results we want, yet we are holding tight to the organizational mindset of the industrial age. It is time to break old bonds, take new journeys, and travel new paths. In the Foreword of this book, Roland Barth, a noted Harvard educator, reminds us that "schools exist to promote the learning of all their inhabitants." He feels that educators should spend most of their time engaged in activities that cause "profound levels" of learning in others. That means that teachers should spend the majority of their time in activities that create peak learning experiences for children; and leaders should spend the majority of their time in activities that create peak learning experiences for everyone in their school or district—children, teachers, and parents.

The fight for learning in our schools should be an easy battle. Yet, when we are talking about fighting for *educators as learners*, the battle is neither easy nor simple. Many questions remain. Where are the time and resources for learning? What is the relationship between collaborative learning communities and student success? How do you sustain the momentum of active, vibrant school-based learning communities? What we need is a continued dialogue among educators to expand our knowledge base about this promising professional development approach. The more voices that contribute, the richer the conversation will become. We invite you to join in.

118

Glossary

Assumption: A theory or belief that provides a rationale for action. For example, an assumption in early childhood education is that young children learn by doing. Based on this assumption, learning environments are designed so that children can be actively engaged with materials and each other.

Capacity building: Developing the human and technological resources within an organization to accomplish its vision and goals.

Charter: An initial documentation of the focus or work of a team. For example, charters for collaborative learning teams might include the team's topic of study, the topic's relationship to the vision of the school, the topic restated in a question, a list of needed resources, and the signature of the administrator.

Collaborative learning model: A school-based or team-based professional development model that promotes collegial inquiry, experimentation, and reflection in areas that are professionally significant to participants and relevant to the vision of the school community.

Collaborative learning process: Interactive learning experiences with two or more people that focus on a topic of interest to the group and contribute to the attainment of the school's vision. The process is cyclical and includes five stages: define, explore, experiment, reflect, and share.

Collaborative learning team: Members of a school community who voluntarily organize themselves into a small group on the basis of their professional interest in the group's topic of study.

Common ground: An idea that resonates among all members of a group; the merging of group opinion around a thought or idea. Common ground is a place of agreement that is reached without forcing or compromising.

Communication norms: Shared expectations about how group members will communicate with each other. Examples of communication norms are listening carefully, sharing relevant information, and developing shared understanding.

Community: A collection of individuals who are organized around relationships and ideas and who choose to come together on the basis of shared purposes, values, ideals, and aspirations.

Consensus: A decision made by a group of individuals where all members perceive they have equal opportunity to influence the decision, and everyone agrees to support the decision.

Core ideology: The enduring character or essence of an organization; the articulation of the purpose and values of an organization.

Core purpose: The focus of the organization; its reason for being or existing.

Core value: A central belief deeply understood and shared by every member of the organization. Core values drive the decisions and guide the actions of everyone in the organization.

Current reality: The internal and external forces that affect the functioning of an organization. In a school, these forces might include the child population, staff expertise, organizational structure, resources, current initiatives, and school culture.

Facilitator: A person who supports the movement of a collaborative learning team toward mutually agreed-on goals and encourages the full participation and valuing of all team members.

Game plan: A blueprint or overview of a group's action plan that is developed prior to beginning action and can be adjusted at any point during the action.

Ground rules: Specific, concrete rules and procedures that guide group functioning. Ground rules provide guidelines for team meeting procedures and a code of conduct for team members.

Group functioning: Ability of the group to perform work, which includes (1) achieving its goal, (2) maintaining good working relationships, and (3) adapting to current circumstances in ways that help the group achieve its goals.

Identity: The unique character of an organization that evolves from multiple aspects of the organization, including its history, values, purpose, current reality, and vision.

Infrastructure: The means or systems through which an organization makes resources available, such as time, money, reward systems, information, management support, and access to colleagues. Alignment should exist between an organization's infrastructure and its purpose, values, and vision.

Interdependence: The perception that one is linked with others in such a way that the success of one depends on the success of others and that the work of each person benefits the whole.

Learning community: Individuals who choose to engage in collaborative learning on the basis of a shared curiosity and a desire to expand their skills and knowledge individually and collectively.

Multiple perspective taking: The ability to see a situation from the point of view of others; the ability to experience the emotional and cognitive reaction of others in a given situation.

Purpose: An organization's reason for being or reason for existing. It is not a goal or a strategy but rather the focus of an organization.

Practice: A strategy or technique that is used to accomplish a specific goal. For example, anecdotal record keeping is an assessment practice, or guided reading is a reading practice.

Process: A method or procedure for doing something; a course of action that often has multiple steps or stages.

Self-organized groups: Groups formed on the basis of shared goals or interests among group members. In self-organized groups, members self-select to be part of a group.

Shared understanding: Two or more individuals reaching a common interpretation of an idea, task, or problem.

Shared vision: A clear, compelling goal that conveys something concrete, visible, and challenging but "doable." It requires thinking beyond the current capabilities of the organization.

Specific measurable results: A description of a specific outcome associated with the school vision that can be observed and measured.

Topic of study: A body of knowledge, skills, strategies, or models that is both (1) meaningful to a group of educators and (2) relevant to the goals and vision of the school.

Tool: An activity that has a specific purpose, a set process, and an anticipated outcome.

References and Bibliography

Bailey, S. (1995). *Forging unified commitment from diverse perspectives: New approaches to helping groups through change.* (ASCD Satellite Broadcast Series). Alexandria, VA: Association for Supervision and Curriculum Development.

Belenky, M. F., Clinchy, B. M., Goldberger, N. R., & Tarule, J. M. (1986). *Women's ways of knowing.* New York: HarperCollins Publishers, Basic Books, Inc.

Bennis, W. (1994). *On becoming a leader.* New York: Addison-Wesley.

Block, P. (1993). *Stewardship.* San Francisco: Berrett-Koehler.

Bohm, D. (1990). *On dialogue.* Ojai, CA: David Bohm Seminars.

Bolin, F. S. (1987). Reassessment and renewal in teaching. In F. S. Bolin & J. M. Falk (Eds.), *Teacher renewal: Professional issues, personal choices* (pp. 1–21). New York: Teachers College Press.

Brandt, R. (1998). *Powerful learning.* Alexandria, VA: Association for Supervision and Curriculum Development.

Brown, A. (1994). The advancement of learning. *Education Research, 23*(8), 4–12.

Caine, R. N., & Caine, G. (1997). *Education on the edge of possibility.* Alexandria, VA: Association for Supervision and Curriculum Development.

Calhoun, E. F. (1993, October). Action research: Three approaches. *Educational Leadership, 51*(2), 62–65.

Carter, M., & Curtis, D. (1994). *Training teachers.* St. Paul: Readleaf Press.

Collins, J., & Porras, J. (1996, March). Building your company's vision. *Harvard Business Review, 74*(2), 65–77.

Covey, S. R. (1989). *The seven habits of highly effective people.* New York: Fireside.

Covey, S. R. (1990). *Principle-centered leadership.* New York: Simon & Schuster.

Darling-Hammond, L. (1997). *The right to learn.* San Francisco: Jossey-Bass.

Darling-Hammond, L. (1996, March). The quiet revolution: Rethinking teacher development. *Educational Leadership, 53*(6), 4–10.

DePree, M. (1987). *Leadership is an art.* San Francisco: Jossey-Bass.

DePree, M. (1997). *Leading without power.* San Francisco: Jossey-Bass.

Fullan, M. G. (1993a). *Change forces: Probing the depths of educational reform.* Bristol, PA: The Falmer Press.

Fullan, M. G. (1993b, March). Why teachers must become change agents. *Educational Leadership, 50*(6), 12–17.

Fullan, M. G. (1995). The school as a learning organization: Distant dreams. *Theory into Practice, 34*(4), 230–235.

Fullan, M. G. (1997). Emotion and hope: Constructive concepts for complex times. In A. Hargreaves (Ed.), *Rethinking educational change with heart and mind* (ASCD 1997 Yearbook, pp. 216–233). Alexandria, VA: Association for Supervision and Curriculum Development.

Fullan, M. G. (1998, April). Breaking the bonds of dependency. *Educational Leadership, 55*(7), 4–9.

Gardner, J. (1964). *Self-renewal.* New York: Harper & Row.

Garmston, R., & Wellman, B. (1998, April).

Teacher talk that makes a difference. *Educational Leadership, 55*(7), 30–34.

The Grove Consultants International. (1995). *Team start up: Creating gameplans for success.* San Francisco: Author.

The Grove Consultants International. (1997). *Process tools for strategic visioning and teams pamphlet.* San Francisco: Author.

Handy, C. (1995). Managing the dream. In S. Chawla & J. Renesch (Eds.), *Learning organizations* (pp. 45–55). Portland, OR: Productivity Press.

Harrison, R. (1995). *The collected papers of Roger Harrison.* San Francisco: Jossey-Bass.

Harvey, E., & Lucia, A. (1997). *144 ways to walk the talk.* Dallas: Performance Publishing Company.

Heider, J. (1985). *The Tao of leadership.* Atlanta: Humanics Limited.

Johnson, D. W., & Johnson, F. P. (1994). *Joining together: Group theory and group skills.* Boston: Allyn & Bacon.

Joyce, B., & Calhoun, E. (1995, April). School renewal: An inquiry, not a formula. *Educational Leadership, 52*(7), 51–55.

Killion, J. P., & Todnem, G. R. (1991, March). A process for personal theory building. *Educational Leadership, 48*(6), 14–16.

Kim, D. H. (1994). Paradigm-creating loops: How paradigms shape reality. In K. T. Wardman (Ed.), *Reflections on creating learning organizations* (pp. 53–60). Cambridge, MA: Pegasus Communications.

Kofman, F., & Senge, P. (1993, Autumn). Communities of commitment: The heart of learning organizations. *Organizational Dynamics, 22*(2), 5–23.

Lieberman, A., & Miller, L. (1990). Teacher development in professional practice schools. *Teacher College Record, 92*(1), 105–121.

Loucks-Horsley, S. (1995). Professional development and the learner-centered school. *Theory into Practice, 34*(4), 236–247.

Lumsden, G., & Lumsden, D. (1993). *Communicating in groups and teams: Sharing leadership.* Belmont, CA: Wadsworth.

Maslow, A. H. (1954). *Motivation and personality.* New York: Harper.

McLaughlin, M., & Talbert, J. E. (1993). *Contexts that matter for teaching and learning.* Stanford, CA: Stanford University.

Nair, K. (1994). *A higher standard of leadership: Lessons from the life of Gandhi.* San Francisco: Berrett-Koehler.

National Commission of Teaching and America's Future (NCTAF). (1996). *What matters most: Teaching for America's future.* New York: Author.

National Foundation for the Improvement of Education (NFIE). (1996). *Teachers take charge of their learning: Transforming professional development for student success.* Washington, DC: Author.

Olson-Ness, J. (1994). *Tools for team building.* Reston, VA: Council for Exceptional Children Inclusive Schools Institute.

O'Neil, J. (1995, April). On schools as learning organizations: A conversation with Peter Senge. *Educational Leadership, 52*(7), 20–23.

Owen, H. (1997). *Expanding our now: The story of open space technology.* San Francisco: Berrett-Koehler.

Peck, S. M. (1987). *The different drum: Community making and peace.* New York: Simon & Schuster.

Prokesch, S. E. (1997, September-October). Unleashing the power of learning: An interview with British Petroleum's John Browne. *Harvard Business Review, 75*(5), 147–168.

Pugach, M. C., & Johnson, L. J. (1995). *Collaborative practitioners: Collaborative schools.* Denver: Love.

Russo, E., & Giblin, C. (1996). *Communication derailed.* King of Prussia, PA: Human Resources Development Quarterly.

Ryan, S. (1994). The emergence of learning communities. In K. T. Wardman (Ed.), *Reflections on creating learning organizations* (pp. 95–105). Cambridge, MA: Pegasus Communications.

Ryan, S. (1995). Learning communities: An alternative to the "expert" model. In S. Chawla & J. Renesch (Eds.), *Learning organizations* (pp. 279–291). Portland, OR: Productivity Press, Inc.

Sagor, R. (1995, April). Overcoming the one-solution syndrome. *Educational Leadership, 52*(7), 24–27.

Saphier, J., & D'Auria, J. (1993). *How to bring vision to school improvement*. Carlisle: MA: Research for Better Teaching, Inc.

Sapon-Shevin, M. (1992). Celebrating Diversity, Creating Community. In S. Stainback & W. Stainback (Eds.), *Curriculum considerations in inclusive classrooms* (pp. 19–36). Baltimore: Paul H. Brookes.

Sarason, S. (1993). *You are thinking of teaching*. San Francisco: Jossey-Bass.

Scannell, E. E., & Newstrom, J. W. (1991). *Still more games trainers play*. New York: McGraw-Hill.

Schaefer, R. J. (1967). *The school as the center of inquiry*. New York: HarperCollins.

Schwahn, C., & Spady, W. (1998). *Total leaders: Applying the best future-focused change strategies to education*. Arlington, VA: American Association of School Administrators.

Schwarz, R. M. (1994). *The skilled facilitator*. San Francisco: Jossey-Bass.

Senge, P. (1990). *The fifth discipline*. New York: Doubleday.

Senge, P., Kleiner, A., Roberts, C., Ross, R., & Smith, B. (1994). *The fifth discipline fieldbook: Strategies and tools for building a learning organization*. New York: Doubleday.

Sergiovanni, T. J. (1996). *Leadership for the schoolhouse*. San Francisco: Jossey-Bass.

Sparks D., & Hirsh, S. (1997). *A new vision for staff development*. Alexandria, VA: Association for Supervision and Curriculum Development.

Uhl, S. C., with Perez-Sellis, M. (1995). The role of collaboration in school transformation: Two approaches. *Theory into Practice, 34*(4), 258–264.

van der Bogert, R. (1998, Spring). Learning in the schoolhouse. *New Directions in School Leadership*, No. 7, 71–83.

Weisbord, M. R., & Janoff, S. (1995). *Future search*. San Francisco: Berrett-Koehler.

Weiss, W. H. (1994, March). Handling communication problems. *Supervision, 55*(3), 17–19.

Wheatley, M. J. (1992). *Leadership and the new science*. San Francisco: Berrett-Koehler.

Wheatley, M. J., & Kellner-Rogers, M. (1996). *A simpler way*. San Francisco: Berrett-Koehler.

Wohlestetter, P., Van Kirk, A., Robertson, P., & Mohrman, S. A. (1997). *Organizing for successful school-based management*. Alexandria, VA: Association for Supervision and Curriculum Development.

Youngblood, M. D. (1997). *Life at the edge of chaos*. Dallas: Perceval Publishing.

Index

acceptance, 62
acquaintance, 31–32
Action Plan Grid, 55 (fig)
  actions, 51–53
  bias, 12
  coordination, 53
active learning, 10–11
activities. *See also* tools
  Action Plan Grid, 55 (fig)
  Appreciative Partner Statements, 65
  Awards Banquet, 40
  Context Mapping, 38, 39 (fig)
  Creating a Team Sculpture, 63
  Current Snapshot, 38, 41 (fig)
  Designer Name Tags, 32
  Exploration Grid, 50, 52 (fig)
  Game Plan, 51 (fig)
  Histomap, 33–34, 35 (fig)
  Individual Reflection, 54
  The Job Game, 32
  Let's String Along, 63
  Magazine Cover Story, 40–41
  Making a Difference, 40
  Moments of Magic, 33 (fig)
  My Treasure Box, 62
  Observations and Interpretations, 55
  Polaroid Pictures, 32
  3–2–1 Reflection, 54
  Say Something About It, 64–65
  Self-disclosure, 62–63
  Similarities and Differences, 62–63
  True Confessions in Four Corners, 32
  Vision Commercial, 40
  What, What, What, 54–55
  What's in It for Me? 32
  What's on My Mind? 65
  Your Calling, 32–33
adaptive learning, 9–10
adult learning, 8–12
Affinity, 85–86
agenda notes, 73 (fig)
always confused, 95
Antrim, Minna, 61 (quoted)
Appreciative Partner Statements, 65
assumptions
  adult learning, 9–12
  community, 13–17
  current, 49–50
  explicit, 67–68
  leadership, 19–20
  learning, 9–12
  new ideas, 50
  questions for examining, 61
  strategies, 68
attention-deficit disorder (ADD), 45, 47–52 (fig)
Awards Banquet, 40

Barth, Roland, v, 118
behaviorists, 60–61
beliefs, questions for examining, 61
Block, Peter, 22
Bohm, D., 66 (quoted), 100 (quoted)
Bolin, F. S., 11 (quoted)
Browne, John, 57

capacity building, 24–25
case study, 26
challenges ahead, 118
change
  efforts, 20
  individual, 116
  need for, 3–4

---

*An index entry followed by "(fig)" indicates an illustration on that page.

roller coaster of, 41–42 (fig)
school community, 116–117
charter, 50 (fig)
children with disabilities, 54 (fig), 117. *See also* peer interaction
collaboration, 15
collaborative learning, 4–5, 59
  communication norms that support, 63–69
  group practices that support, 69–74
collaborative learning process, 44, 46 (fig)–47. *See also* learning process
  defining, 47–49
  experimenting, 51–53
  exploring, 49–51
  reflecting, 53–56
  sharing, 56–58
  stages, 47–58
  time line, 47 (fig)
collaborative learning teams, 44
  case study, 45
  challenges to, 118
  influence on instructional practice, 117
  and leadership style, 118
  and results, 118
  schoolwide focus, 117
  time requirements, 117
collaborative work discussion, questions, 57, 58
collective mind, 25
Collins, J., 41 (quoted)
communication norms, 63–69
Communication Norms for Collaborative Groups, 92–102
  Decide by Consensus, 68–69, 102
  Develop Shared Meaning, 66–67, 100
  fact sheets, 98–102
  Listen Carefully, 64–65, 98
  Make Assumptions Explicit, 67–68, 101
  role cards, 95–97
  Share Relevant Information, 66, 99
Communication Patterns, 112–115 (fig)
community, 13–17
  concept, 31
  compromiser, 72 (fig)
consensus, 67
  decision by, 68–69
  strategies to test for, 69
constructivists, 61
Context Mapping, 38, 39 (fig)
contributors, 124–125
cooperative intention, 62
core purpose, 36, 39

core values, 36–37
Covey, Stephen, 26–27, 59 (quoted)
Creating a Team Sculpture, 63
creative solutions, 61–63
Crossroads Elementary School, case study, 28
Current Snapshot, 38, 41 (fig)

D'Aura, J., 36 (quoted)
Darling-Hammond, L., 10, 44, 46 (quoted)
Decided by Consensus, 102
defining, collaborative learning process, 47–49
DePree, Max, 20, 24 (quoted)
Designer Name Tags, 32
designing an experiment, questions, 56
Develop Shared Meaning, 100
Dewey, John, 9
didactic talking, 63–64
diversity, 14–15, 34
documenting results, questions, 56

editors, 124
effective teaching, 16
Eliot, T. S., 18 (quoted)
encourager, 72 (fig)
expectations, shared, 63
experimental learning, 11–12. *See also* collaborative learning process
Exploration Grid, 50, 52 (fig)
exploring, collaborative learning process, 49–51

facilitator, 71 (fig)
family involvement, 117
The Fifth Discipline Fieldbook, 61, 64 (quoted), 65
Force Field Analysis, 38, 79–81
Fullan, Michael, 13, 16 (quoted)

game plan, 49
Game Plan, 51 (fig)
Gandhi, 20, 22
  Lessons from the Life of Gandhi, 19, 22
Gardner, John, 5–6 (quoted)
gatekeeper, 70, 72 (fig)
generative learning, 9–10
ground rules
  brainstorming, sample, 70 (fig)
  establishing, 69–70
  meetings, sample, 70 (fig)
Ground Rules, 109–111
group practices
  Document Information, 71
  Establish Ground Rules, 69–70

Explore Trust and Task Roles, 70
Reflect on Group Processes, 71–72
group process
  reflection, 71–72
  questions, 56, 57

Handy, C., 10
Harvey, E., 22
Hayward Elementary School, case study
  Action Plan Grid, 55 (fig)
  collaborative learning, 45
  KWL Chart, 54 (fig)
  Shared Meaning Chart, 49 (fig)
  shared meaning, 48
Heider, John, 19–20 (quoted), 22–23 (quoted)
Histomapping, 33–34, 35 (fig)
history, 33–34

ideology, core, 34, 36–37
inclusion, 117
individual
  change, 116
  reflection, questions, 57
information
  documenting, 71
  dissemination, 71
  sharing, 66
information-fueled learning, 12
inquiry into underlying assumptions, learning
  process and, 9–10
inservice approach, 7–8
instructional practices, 117
interdependence, 15, 59–63

The Job Game, 32
judgment, 62

Kellner-Rogers, Myron, 14 (quoted), 15 (quoted),
  27, 57–58 (quoted)
Killion, J. P., 53 (quoted)
Kim, Daniel, 9
know-it-all, 97
Kofman, F., 14 (quoted), 16 (quoted)
Krishnamurti, Jiddu, 64 (quoted)
KWL Chart, 50, 54 (fig)

Lakeside Elementary School, case study, 25
leader
  capacity-building and, 24
  hero, as, 26
  relationship-building and, 26

leadership, 18, 19
  assumptions, 19–20
  service-based, 22–23
  style, 118
  values, 20, 22
  vision, 20, 21
Leadership and the New Sciences, 14
Leadership for the Schoolhouse, 8
Leading Without Power, 20
learning, 60–61
  learner-driven, 11
  reframed, vii
learning communities, 15–16
learning disabilities (LD), 21
learning process. See also collaborative learning
  process
  active, 10–11
  adaptive, 9–10
  experimental, 11–12
  generative, 9–10
  information-fueled, 12
  learner-driven, around meaningful issues, 11
Left-Hand Column, 103–106
Lessons from the Life of Gandhi, 19, 22
Let's String Along, 63
Life at the Edge of Chaos, 3
limited English proficiency (LEP), in children, 21,
  23
Listen Carefully, 98
listening, 64, 65
Lucia, A., 22

Magazine Cover Story, 40–41
Make Assumptions Explicit, 101
Making a Difference, 40
Making Learning Communities Work, 27–28
Maslow, Abraham, 26
mechanistic imagery, 3
mild mental retardation (MR), 45
Moments of Magic, 33 (fig)
motivation to learn, 11
My Treasure Box, 62

Nair, Keshavan, 19 (quoted), 22 (quoted)
National Commission of Teaching and America's
  Future, 19
National Foundation for Improvement in Education (NFIE), 8
new ideas, 50
  questions for exploring, 53
  ways to look for, 50

A New Vision for Staff Development, 27

Oakwood Elementary School, case study, 26
Observations and Interpretations, 55
obstacles to learning, 12
off topic, 97
144 Ways to Walk the Talk, 22
on-the-job learning, 11
Open Space, 87–90
openness, 62
others, understanding, 61–63

Peck, S. M., 13 (quoted)
peer interaction, 52–55 (fig), 57
perspectives, sharing, 32–33
philosophy, shared, 13–14
Polaroid Pictures, 32
Porras, J., 41 (quoted)
poster session, 57
potential, unpredictable, 15–16
practices
   current, 49–50
   group, 69–72
   instructional, 117
   questions about, 50
principal as leader, 21, 22, 23, 25, 26, 27, 28, 45
Principle-Centered Leadership, 26–27
Probable and Preferred Future, 82–84
process, 29
professional development in schools, 4–5
professional growth, areas for, 44
professional learning communities, 5 (fig)
Project REALIGN, viii
protector, 96
purpose, 14
   core, 36
   how to articulate, 36
The Pyramid, 107–108

questions
   beliefs and assumptions, 61
   collaborative learning, reflecting on, 58
   collaborative work, discussion, 58
   current practices, 50
   designing an experiment, 56
   documenting results, 56
   group reflection, 57, 72
   Histomap, 34
   individual reflection, 57
   new ideas, 53
   professional growth areas, 44

refining questions, 51
refining team question, 56
self-understanding, 59, 62
sharing insights, 56
team question, 54 (fig)
topic formulation, 48
vision, 39

REALIGN, viii, 116
reality, assessing, 38
really talking, 63–64
recorder, 71, 71 (fig)
references, 121–123
reflection
   collaborative learning process, 53–56
   collaborative learning process, questions, 58
   group, 55–56
   group questions, 56, 57, 72
   individual, 54–55
   individual questions, 57
   3–2–1 Reflection, 54
   reflector, 72 (fig)
relationship building, 26–27
   case study, 28
resources, 12
results
   observation and documentation, 53
   sharing, 118
Roberts, Charlotte, 61
roller coaster of change, 41–42 (fig)

Sagor, R., 56 (quoted)
Sanford Elementary School, values case study, 23
Saphier, J., 36 (quoted)
Sarason, S., 43 (quoted)
Say Something About It, 64–65
schools
   as communities, 4–5
   community change, 116–117
   improvement plan, 43
   schoolwide focus, 117
Schwahn, Charles, 23–24 (quoted), 68 (quoted), 69 (quoted), 102 (quoted)
Self-disclosure, 62–63
Self-Renewal, 5–6
self-understanding, 60–61
   questions for, 59
Senge, Peter, 9, 14 (quoted), 16 (quoted), 20 (quoted), 98 (quoted)
Sergiovanni, Thomas, 8 (quoted), 11, 16 (quoted), 23

service, 22–23
  case study, 25
Share Relevant Information, 99
shared meaning
  developing, 66–67
  promoting, 48
  strategies, 67
Shared Meaning Chart, 48, 49 (fig)
shared philosophy, 13–14
shared vision, 39–41
sharing, 56–58, 62
  insights, questions, 56
  results, 118
Similarities and Differences, 62–63
A Simpler Way, 57–58
Spady, William, 23–24 (quoted)
special education, 21
staff development plan, 43–44
  professional growth areas, 44
  strategic plan, 43
strategies
  assumptions, making explicit, 68
  consensus testing, 69
  listening carefully, 65
  promoting shared meaning, 48
  shared meaning, developing, 67
summarizer, 70, 71 (fig)
support, 62
synergy, 15, 58

The Tao of Leadership, 19–20, 22–23
task roles, 70, 71 (fig)
Teachers Take Charge of Their Learning, 8, 11
  (quoted)
team functioning scale, 73 (fig)
team question, refining, 56
Think, Pair, Share, 91
time, 117
time line, collaborative learning process, 47 (fig)
timekeeper, 71 (fig)
Todnem, G. R., 53 (quoted)
tools for learning, 75, 77, 79–114. See also activities
  Affinity, 85–86
  Communication Norms for Collaborative Groups,
    92–102
  Communication Patterns, 112–115 (fig)
  Force Field Analysis, 38, 79–81
  Ground Rules, 109–111

Left-Hand Column, 103–106
Open Space, 87–90
Probable and Preferred Future, 82–84
The Pyramid, 107–108
Think, Pair, Share, 91
topics. See also questions
  charter, 50 (fig)
  defining, 47–48
  sharing, 49
Total Leaders, 23–24
traditional training, 7–8
Tragore, Rabindranath, 3 (quoted)
training food chain, 7–8
tree image (Current Snapshot), 38, 41
True Confessions in Four Corners, 32
trust, 59, 62
"trust" roles, 70, 72 (fig)
trusting environments, 62

Uhl, S. C., 16 (quoted)

values, 14, 20, 22
  case study, 23
  core, 36–37
van der Bogert, Rebecca, 27–28 (quoted)
vision, 14, 20, 117
  case study, 21, 45
  creating, 39–42
Vision Commercial, 40
Votjek, Rosie O'Brian, 27 (quoted)

144 Ways to Walk the Talk, 22
weaver analogy, 18
Westlake Elementary School, vision case study, 21
What Matters Most: Teaching for America's Future,
  19 (quoted)
What, What, What, 54–55
What's in It for Me? 32
What's on My Mind? 65
Wheatley, Margaret, 12 (quoted), 14 (quoted),
  15 (quoted), 27, 57–58 (quoted)
wheel of learning, 10–11 (fig)
withholder (silent but knowing), 95
worldview, 60

"yes" person, 96
Youngblood, M. D., 3 (quoted)
Your Calling, 32–33

About the Editors and Contributors

Editors

Penelope J. Wald has taught and consulted in the field of education for three decades. Her teaching experience ranges from elementary general and special education to the graduate school level. From 1988 to 1999 Wald has been a member of the research staff at The George Washington University Graduate School of Education and Human Development and served as Project Director for three federally funded model projects focused on quality inclusive education. She is a coauthor, with Marie Abraham and Lori Morris, of *Inclusive Early Childhood Education* (Communication Skill Builders, 1993). She has consulted with the U.S. Agency for International Development's Egypt Training Project and the U.S. Department of Education, as well as local, state, and national programs on issues of early childhood inclusion and building professional learning communities. She can be reached at 402 N. View Terrace, Alexandria, VA 22301. Telephone: 703-549-9690. E-mail: pwald@erols.com

Michael S. Castleberry, Professor of Special Education at The George Washington University, has taught at the undergraduate, master's, and doctoral levels and has been active in sponsored activities related to teacher preparation in early childhood special education. His teaching emphasis is in the area of developmental assessment and testing, behavior management, and professional staff development. During his 26 years at the university, he has consulted with the U.S. Department of Defense, the Department of the Treasury, Project HOPE, and school systems throughout the Washington, D.C., area. His current interest is in the establishment of professional development schools with area school districts. He can be reached at the Department of Teacher Preparation and Special Education, The George Washington University, 2134 G Street, N.W., Washington, DC 20052. Telephone: 202-994-1510. E-mail: castle@gwu.edu

Contributors

Laura Bell, Early Childhood Educator, Fairfax County (Virginia) Public Schools, and Facilitator for Project REALIGN. Bell contributed to Chapter 6, "Enhancing the Capacity to Learn." She can be reached at 11902 Triple Crown Rd., Reston, VA 20191.

Holly Blum, Early Childhood Curriculum and Inclusion Specialist, Fairfax County (Virginia)

Public Schools, and team member of Project REALIGN. Blum contributed to Chapter 3, "Leading Professional Learning Communities," and Chapter 5, "Learning as a Community." She can be reached at 9463 Cloverdale Ct., Burke, VA 22015.

Amy King, Early Childhood Special Educator, Fairfax County (Virginia) Public Schools, and Facilitator for Project REALIGN. King contributed to Chapter 4, "Identity of the Learning Community," and was the coteacher (with Ramona Wright) of a district staff development course entitled "Staff as Collaborative Learners: Creating Quality Programs for Children with Diverse Needs." She can be reached at 306 Ralston Rd., Richmond, VA 23229.

Andrea Sobel, Training Specialist, Project REALIGN, The George Washington University. Sobel contributed to Chapter 4, "Identity of the Learning Community," Chapter 6, "Enhancing Capacity to Learn," and Part III, "Tools for Learning." She can be reached at

8328 The Midway, Annandale, VA 22003.

Maret Wahab, Early Childhood Special Educator, Fairfax County (Virginia) Public Schools, and team member of Project REALIGN. Wahab contributed to Chapter 4, "Identity of the Learning Community." She can be reached at 6629 Claymore Ct., McLean, VA 22101.

Karen Ikeda Wood, educational consultant and team member of Project REALIGN. Wood contributed to Chapter 6, "Enhancing the Capacity to Learn." She can be reached at 11432 South 44th St., Phoenix, AZ 85044.

Ramona Wright, Early Childhood Special Educator, Fairfax County (Virginia) Public Schools, and Facilitator, Project REALIGN. Wright contributed to Chapter 5, "Learning as a Community," and was coteacher (with Amy King) of a staff development course, "Staff as Collaborative Learners." She can be reached at 10906 Harpers Square Ct., Reston, VA 20191-5011.

Related ASCD Resources: Building a Professional Learning Community

Audiotapes

Building a Community of Researchers to Improve Practice (live recording from the 1999 ASCD Annual Conference)

Creating Learning Communities by Anne Bryant

Elements of Successful Staff Development: The Principal's Role (live recording from the 1999 ASCD Annual Conference

Urban Professional Development Initiative Retreat (live recordings of ASCD retreat for urban school leaders by Stephanie Hirsh and Joellen Killion)

Staff Development for Increasing Teacher Effectiveness and Student Achievement by Ann Wood

CD-ROM

Educational Leadership CD-ROM

Online Articles

"Professional Development: The Linchpin of Teacher Quality," by Brian Sullivan (*Infobrief*) (URL: http://ascd.org/issues/professional_development.html)

"Teacher, Improve Thyself: A Call for Self-Reliant, Reflective Practitioners," by Carol Bunting (*Classroom Leadership Online*) (URL: http://www.ascd.org/pubs/cl/1aug99.html)

"Teacher Learning That Supports Student Learning," by Linda Darling-Hammond (*Educational Leadership*) (URL: http://www.ascd.org/pubs/el/feb98/extdarl.htm)

Online Course

Effective Leadership (PD Online Course) (URL: http://www.ascd.org/pdi/pd.html)

Print Products

Building Leadership Capacity in Schools by Linda Lambert

Changing School Culture Through Staff Development (1990 ASCD Yearbook) edited by Bruce Joyce

The Hero's Journey: How Educators Can Transform Schools and Improve Learning by John L. Brown and Cerylle A. Moffett

How to Organize a School-Based Staff Development Program by Fred Wood

A New Vision for Staff Development by Dennis Sparks and Stephanie Hirsh

Professional Learning Communities at Work: Best Practices for Enhancing Student Achievement by Richard DuFour and Robert Eaker

Strengthening the Teaching Profession, *Educational Leadership*, Vol. 55, No. 5, February 1998

Videotapes

The Principal Series: Tape 2: Creating A Collaborative Learning Community (45 minute videotape plus Facilitator's Guide)

Schools As Communities: Teachers and Students Build a Successful School Community (30-minute videotape plus Facilitator's Guide)

For additional resources, visit us on the World Wide Web (http://www.ascd.org), send an e-mail message to member@ascd.org, call the ASCD Service Center (1-800-933-ASCD or 703-578-9600, then press 2), send a fax to 703-575-5400, or write to Information Services, ASCD, 1703 N. Beauregard St., Alexandria, VA 22311-1714 USA.